W9-DFV-141

Human Learning

THE STUDENTS LIBRARY OF EDUCATION

GENERAL EDITOR:

J. W. Tibble
Emeritus Professor of Education
University of Leicester

EDITORIAL BOARD:

Psychology of Education:
Professor Ben Morris
University of Bristol

Philosophy of Education:
Professor Richard S. Peters
Institute of Education
University of London

History of Education:
Professor Brian Simon
University of Leicester

Sociology of Education:
Professor William Taylor
Department of Education
University of Bristol

Volumes dealing with curriculum studies, methodology
and other more general topics are the responsibility of
the General Editor, Professor Tibble.

Human Learning:
a Developmental Analysis

by H. S. N. McFarland
Professor of Education
University of Durham

Library
Southwestern State College
Weatherford, Okla.
Weatherford, Oklahoma

LONDON
ROUTLEDGE & KEGAN PAUL
NEW YORK: HUMANITIES PRESS

First published 1969
by Routledge & Kegan Paul Ltd
Broadway House, 68-74 Carter Lane, E.C.4
Printed in Great Britain by
Northumberland Press Limited
Gateshead
© H. S. N. McFarland 1969
No part of this book may be reproduced
in any form without permission from
the publisher, except for the quotation
of brief passages in criticism.
SBN 7100 6427 6 (c)
SBN 7100 6428 4 (p)

THE STUDENTS LIBRARY OF EDUCATION has been designed to meet the needs of students of Education at Colleges of Education and at University Institutes and Departments. It will also be valuable for practising teachers and educationists. The series takes full account of the latest developments in teacher-training and of new methods and approaches in education. Separate volumes will provide authoritative and up-to-date accounts of the topics within the major fields of sociology, philosophy and history of education, educational psychology, and method. Care has been taken that specialist topics are treated lucidly and usefully for the non-specialist reader. Altogether, the Students' Library of Education will provide a comprehensive introduction and guide to anyone concerned with the study of education, and with educational theory and practice.

J. W. TIBBLE

As a phenomenon and as a concept, learning, would seem to be central to the study of education. Indeed the psychological literature on learning is immense. Yet paradoxically it is difficult to find satisfactory introductory studies of human learning which have a direct appeal to teachers, and to students of education. There would appear to be two main reasons for this. The first is that most of the work on learning in general, is in terms of simpler species than *homo sapiens* and is not significantly relevant to the kinds of learning with which education is concerned. The second is that the various approaches to the study of human learning which are of potential relevance for education require considerable interpretative skill for their relevance to be clearly appreciated. Moreover the exercise of this skill has to start from the assumption that the relevance sought is for the most part not directly instrumental or prescriptive but rather lies in an enlargement of conceptual understanding.

Professor McFarland's book offers to teachers the kind of scholarship and interpretative skill essential to this task. At the outset he makes clear how complex a phenomenon human learning is, and how many sided are the approaches

v

which have to be made to its study for this complexity to be grasped. Throughout he stresses the fact that since 'learning' is to be thought of as an intrinsic component of the more general idea of 'development', it has always to be seen in a developmental perspective. Such an approach also has the advantage that it allows the institutional settings within which learning takes place to be considered as essential factors in the process. Hence, the treatment of pre-school learning, primary-school learning. and secondary-school learning becomes the major conceptual framework for the book.

These virtues apart, what seems to me particularly refreshing about Professor McFarland's approach is his insistence that 'learning' is a controversial topic and that a vast amount of agreed wisdom is not to be obtained at present in this field. Moreover he concludes not by summarizing what is known but by reiterating some of the basic questions about learning, questions which by their very nature may require different answers in different contexts and at different times.

BEN MORRIS

Contents

CONTENTS

1

Introduction: Some aspects of student learning and some approaches to the analysis of learning

The meaning of learning

How does one learn about learning? The student of learning must be engaged in the very process he wants to study. Can he, so to speak, catch himself in the act? Or are there so many acts in which he may catch himself that he would still be unable to say what learning is? He might find himself reading this book, writing up a scientific experiment, solving a mathematical problem, revising the rough draft of an essay, arguing a point with a friend, exercising his German during a visit abroad, climbing a rock face, tinkering with his car engine, attending an interview, striving for the favour of a beautiful girl, or any of a still greater variety of activities in which one is both learning and, in a sense, learning how one learns. If the attempt to catch oneself red-handed in the act of learning proves too confusing or frustrating, it may still suggest at least one thing—that learning is a rather varied and complex thing.

Webster's Collegiate Dictionary sums up common usage of the word *learn* in the phrase 'to gain knowledge or understanding of or skill in by study, instruction, or experience'. This definition brings to mind some of the kinds of achievement that learning may signify and the means available for the achievement. The word 'gain' is important, emphasizing, as it does, change in understanding or skill. Although it can be said that one learns all the time, much thinking and behaviour is thoroughly habitual, and much of the variation from habit is of a minor or temporary character. The criterion of relative permanence entered into R. S. Woodworth's definition of learning as 'any activity that produces a relatively permanent effect on later activity' (Woodworth, 1940). Psychologists of the behaviourist school sometimes prefer a definition like that given by P. H. Mussen—'the establishment of a connection or association between a stimulus and a response where, prior to learning, no such association existed' (Mussen, 1956). Although this is meant to be more specific and scientific, its neat abstraction covers up many conflicting interpretations, and is challenged also as being intrinsically inadequate to give a complete explanation of learning. Godfrey Vesey is one of those who have, on logical grounds, challenged this assimilation of learning to conditioning, saying that 'whatever one does, in learning to do something, must itself be really something one *does*, something in which one is actively engaged. It cannot be simply something which happens to one' (Peters, 1967). And a more general stress on a non-mechanical view of learning occurs in Michael Oakeshott's statement: 'By learning I mean an activity possible only to an intelligence capable of choice and self-direction in relation to his own impulses and to the world around him' (Peters, 1967).

The variety and complexity of learning phenomena seems to be matched by the variety and complexity of definitions offered for the very concept of learning. One way out of this variety and complexity may be to look around for examples of simpler learning that may give the essential clue to what learning is. But, of course, complex learning may operate quite differently from simple learning. It may be that the huge amount of experimental work with cats, dogs, chimpanzees, white rats, worms, pigeons and the rest of the laboratory menagerie tells us something about how these animals learn but little about how human beings learn. If our sense of biological evolution makes us feel that there must be some link between simple animal learning and complex human learning, we may still suspect that man is so much more than the proverbial 'monkey shaved' that he needs at least some learning laws of his own beyond those that operate in the menagerie. Even if the brightest monkeys are sometimes distressingly like the dullest man, we still have to accommodate human intellectual achievements which really do not invite categorization along with monkey tricks. Although it would be folly to ignore so much fascinating and illuminating work, let us perversely persist in looking a little further at learning in the complex, confusing forms that it takes in the activities of students in colleges and universities. One may consider *en route* whether a student-centred approach to learning is as profitable as a child-centred approach is often alleged to be in schools.

Five aspects of student learning

What does an individual student bring with him as he enters upon his higher education (tertiary education, as it is sometimes now called)? Some conception of his own achievement and potentiality, shaped by his performance and reputation at school and by the standing of the institution of higher education which has favoured him with admission. Some sense of a particular academic, and perhaps professional, aptitude and orientation, varying from a general taste for, let us say, history, because it has been found interesting, to something vocationally specific, such as a firm decision to read medicine and become a doctor. Some sense of his own personality and interests—varying degrees of sociability or reserve, of tough-mindedness or sensitivity, of attraction to serious pursuits or to fun-and-games, of being a solid slogger or a bright-boy or even a clever-dick; varying interests, from electronics to womanizing, from railways to madrigals, from setting the fashion trends to bouncing on the trampoline, from rugby to chess. Some sense of feeling more at ease with one social group than another—perhaps, in the beginning, with the former pupils of one's own school or home district rather than with others, with former fee-paying pupils rather than the former pupils of maintained schools (or vice versa), with arts or social science 'types' rather than with medicos or engineers, with northerners rather than southerners, or with the English rather than the Scots. Some expectation of what higher education will be like—a too ecstatic expectation that builds up for a disappointment, or an apprehensive expectation that will shortly be dispelled by reassurance; an expectation of schoolmasterly solicitude which may confront professorial detachment, or an expectation of glorious freedom which may have to confront tutorial concern and insistence.

Although a student still has a lot to learn about himself (who has not?), his conception of himself is already far developed and is correlated at least in some measure with what he really is, or, to avoid metaphysical speculation, what many mature and experienced persons will see him as being. The don, and later the potential employer, who interview or otherwise assess him will match against their own experience the signs in the student of intelligence, background, academic achievement, character, interests, and personality, displayed in behaviour, appearance, discourse, and accumulated records. Higher education should, and mostly does, make a difference to a person's knowledge, skills, and attitudes, but, of course, many fundamental capacities and attitudes have become rather permanently defined in the upbringing of almost two decades preceding entry upon higher education. Without making too much of the silk-purses-and-sows'-ears argument, one has still to recognize that some of the conditions of learning in higher education are limitations intrinsic to the learner and his earlier experience. Where these limitations have been imposed by handicaps of circumstance or by the establishment of a mistakenly humble self-concept, higher education can, of course, sometimes do wonders. There is, however, a corresponding group of students whose self-concept may suffer deflation and whose limitations may be more stubbornly resistant to modification. For the purpose of the present argument, what matters is that one tremendous aspect of higher learning is the great variety of achievement and capacity represented even among the select proportion of the whole population who are privileged to embark upon higher education. It will not be surprising if the great extent of individual variation is a persistent feature when one looks at the learning of other age groups and at less highly selected sections of the general population.

How does learning vary with what has to be learned? This is a second main question that can be asked in the context of higher education, and some answers suggest themselves very easily. Reading lots of books, as one must in subjects like English and history, is rather different from concentrating on a few text books, as one might do for some courses in science or technology. Working regularly in laboratories is a different activity, teaching one different skills, from essay-writing or seminar discussion. Solving mathematical problems is different from teaching mathematics to schoolchildren. Pursuing a school subject, like geography or French, at the more advanced level of university study is different from embarking on a subject one has never studied at school, such as Persian or philosophy or political science. One could extend such obvious illustrations, but it is more important to mention that these differences are not just technical differences among different areas of knowledge and academic skills. Along with the technical differences there are commonly major differences of atmosphere, so that the scientist comes to feel that learning is something you do in laboratories with benches and apparatus, the student of literature that learning means reading and writing essays, the medical student that learning is working in clinics and hospitals, the student of education that it is working in schools.

These distinctive atmospheres of learning become almost indissociable from the meaning of learning for the various classes of learner. This is well illustrated in graduate classes in education, where scientists have sometimes a limited sense of science as a set of attitudes and principles that can be taken and used outside the subject laboratory, and arts graduates sometimes lack a sense of how literature or history can illuminate a broader area of life than is represented by a set of final honours examination papers. Perhaps more expectedly, the scientist may shy off the uncertainties of imprecise human situations, despite the intrinsic uncertainties at the boundaries of scientific study; and the arts graduate off the mildly precise probabilities of statistical analysis, despite the increasing precision of scholarly study in the arts.

Apart from these atmospheric effects attached to particular studies because of the nature of the studies themselves, there are similar effects which draw on wider and perhaps more potent forces. One of these is the status of any class of institution in society. The longer an institution has enjoyed and merited high esteem the more does it tend to attract the ablest people, who in turn tend to confirm the institution's status. Universities, for example, have tended to enjoy a higher status than other institutions of higher education, and, among universities, some have stood out among the rest even in our own egalitarian times. One thinks of Oxford and Cambridge, Paris, Moscow, or certain United States universities. Age is not essential to high status, but, where a new institution attains to high status rapidly, there may well be a concatenation of highly favourable circumstances, some of them linking newly thought-out ways of operation with high-status elements from an older system. The longer an institution has enjoyed low status the more difficult is it to live down this reputation and build up a new one. The history of colleges of education (formerly called 'training colleges') illustrates this problem and, fortunately, in more recent times, the possibility of improving a poor position through expansion, reorganization, and reformation of aims and methods. For the purpose of the present argument, the detailed operation of these factors does not matter, although it is a most interesting area of study (see Marris, 1964 or Sanford, 1962). What does matter is the fact that there are such factors and that they persistently and subtly shape students' feelings about what learning is possible and how important it is. The shaping, although subtle, is not intangible. It takes place through the substantial character of the people, the buildings, the curricula, the syllabuses, the societies, the bookshops, the music and drama, and all the other things with which one lives. And institutions could be arranged along a scale, from those that extend a student's sense of learning widely in many directions to those which may leave him not even aware of certain dimensions of learning.

In addition to this atmospheric effect on learning of individual institutions or of classes of institution, subjects of study themselves can be viewed as institutions with common interests vested in particular groups of teachers, buildings, curricula, books and periodicals, jargons, career possibilities, academic and professional associations, and so on. The humble student must find his learning influenced, at least marginally, by this aspect of the world of learning. In one generation classics is the only fit study for an able man; in another generation the physical sciences reign supreme; in another, social sciences are

7

battling for a place in the sun and the world of learning is a supermarket with each commodity competing to catch the customer's eye. Here are education or medicine or engineering, assured of their professional utility; there is mathematics, so generally indispensable that mathematicians can be allowed to ignore (or feign to ignore) immediate utilities. Here are the languages and literatures striving to keep old traditions of humane study alive, and there are psychology and economics and sociology trying to substitute their own interpretations of humanity or to entrench themselves within the respectability of the scientific camp. It might be difficult to establish whether the clash of subject with subject does more to cross-fertilize ideas in the student's mind or to transmit the narrowing jealousies of subject specialists.

The learner himself, the subject of study, and the institutions of learning have now been mentioned. Two more major factors of learning have to be mentioned—teaching and techniques of study. A great deal has been written about university teaching and it is possible only to mention a few points about its relation to learning. One might mention first of all that the variables are many and complex and not susceptible of easy measurement in many cases. A list of standard teaching methods would include dispensing guidance and directions about reading; defining areas to be studied through curricula and syllabuses or through learning programmes; commenting on written work; supervising tutorial or seminar discussions; arranging and supervising laboratory work, field work, industrial experience, language experience overseas, school teaching practice, clinical apprenticeship, hospital internships, and other forms of practical experience and training; lecturing; testing and examining (which are often as much teaching methods as assessment methods); and providing general informal advice about studies and related matters on miscellaneous occasions. Any one of these teaching methods means a huge variety of different things in practice—depending on the subject of study, the mind and personality of teacher and of student, the tradition and current bias of the university or college, the general character of the examination structure, and, doubtless, many other things. Thus one may talk about lecturing as one form of teaching, but it is also one hundred and one or one thousand and one different forms.

With so much complexity, it is perhaps not surprising that there is little conclusive evidence demonstrating the superiority of any one teaching method over any other in achieving a particular educational aim. Not only are factors of personality and circumstance difficult to assess or control, but the aims themselves are very varied (perhaps rightly so). Even superficially similar aims are often quite different in effect. Moreover, the aims of higher education, even when they are narrowed down to an academic specification for a particular subject and stage of study, are apt to be intrinsically complex, difficult to assess with high statistical reliability, and subject to different emphases by equally reputable specialists. Knowledge that certain techniques of assessment are imperfect does not necessarily cause people to modify those techniques. Sometimes this is just persistence in bad ways but sometimes it is the felt necessity of accepting an imperfect but available device because a conceivably better one is not genuinely available. The interview, with its plausibility and yet well demonstrated unreliability, is an example. While it may be too easy to slip into a reactionary defence of well-established institutions such as lectures or examinations or interviews, it is necessary to try and consider why such institutions persist, particularly when they do so in countries or areas with radically different traditions, or in newly established colleges which have deliberately tried to be up to date or ahead of their time.

If direct proof about teaching methods is not in large

supply, indirect evidence of various kinds still deserves mention. For example, whatever the imperfections of current methods and however little they contribute to actual learning (as distinct from pretending to learn by various attendances and pseudo-performances), it is difficult to believe that students would learn as much as they genuinely do if their teachers did *none* of the teaching that they do. Furthermore, the common belief of students and teachers, supported by plausible psychological principles, that one can learn better where one does and experiences things for oneself, as distinct from hearing or reading an account of them, would seem to justify considerable emphasis on this kind of active learning. This is said without prejudice to the desirability of developing an active skill in using other people's accounts. A third point is that a method such as lecturing may achieve most if it is not overdone—if it does not become a pouring out, hour after hour, of more information than the student can note down, let alone understand or remember. Excessive lecturing characterizes some areas of higher study—particularly where teachers fail to solve the admittedly difficult problem of restructuring the syllabus as the quantity of usable knowledge grows.

A fourth factor that clearly shapes learning in a vital and controllable way is the system of assessment or examining, viewed here as a virtual teaching method. Weekly quiz, termly examination, regularly assessed laboratory records, dissertation, ten-minute paper for the seminar or *travail de longue haleine* for the Finals—these and other varieties of performance have a most direct influence on patterns of student learning, disposing students to different distributions of time and effort. A skilful teacher would presumably deploy these various methods to make the best use of the typical student's eagerness to do what is necessary for success, while encouraging a growing attitude of interest in studies for their own sake as well as for the academic accolade which they eventually earn.

But perhaps more important than any methods of teaching in the senses mentioned above are subtler aspects of method—a variety of ways in which admittedly good teachers capture the respect and allegiance of their students. Sheer intellectual power (sometimes without any other particular attraction) may be its own pedagogic method, at any rate for some students. Genuine concern for students, however manifest, is another ingredient of effective teaching. And a sense of humour and common humanity is a third. While such factors can be labelled 'personality' and considered beyond human control, this is perhaps too fatalistic an attitude. Intellectual power can be developed by study and even a humourless detachment of temperament be at least moderated by social self-commitment. In higher education, where there will always be a special premium on intellectual and academic achievement, it is impractical to think in terms of perfecting pedagogic skills in themselves. The pedagogy is particularly inextricable from the substance of the learning to be done and teachers will always have to be wooed into reflecting from time to time on the practicability of specific limited improvements in technique. The United States has long done much more than the United Kingdom in devising training programmes for junior university teachers, and these probably have a certain limited value, but the common imperfections still persist. Moreover, large proportions of students simply do not have contact with the most outstanding scholars but are left to the mercies of junior instructors who, however pedagogically trained, are still just junior instructors.

The preceding paragraphs just touch the problem of teaching and learning, but there is the other approach from the side of the learner himself. How do the learner's study techniques influence the process of higher learning? As in the case of teaching, there are some technical principles, commonly mentioned in guides to study (see Maddox, 1963), and there are subtler aspects of the economy of study which have to do with a student's ability, temperament, habits, and self-concept. The technical principles might include such precepts as taking care to find out what and where are the library and other learning resources of a college; spacing out one's learning rather than cramming it into a short period (although realists now admit that some students do pass some examinations by last-minute cramming); trying to recall actively what one is required to learn rather than just reading it repeatedly in a book or in notes; 'over-learning' material that is of exceptional importance; talking over topics and problems with colleagues rather than going it alone in exclusively private study; taking notes that would be intelligible to another person—and, therefore, intelligible to the 'other person' that oneself has become a few months after taking them; preparing and adhering to a realistic work schedule in which working periods, however modest, are used for real work, and regular leisure periods are free from the pangs of work-conscience; or using vacation study to give oneself a head-start on the next session or to fill in the gaps of the preceding session. Some students may succeed in defiance of such precepts; some may believe the precepts but fail to act on them; some may mistake which precepts are particularly relevant to their own situation. But the precepts are not arbitrary. Some have the support of psychological research, others are at least cautionary tautologies (for example, that unintelligible notes will be unintelligible!). Tutors, librarians, organizers of freshers' conferences, and others who may impart advice on the themes just mentioned are helping to prevent waste through ignorance, although they cannot, at one go, ensure that the imparted advice sticks. This depends on the continuing personal guidance of tutors and on the structure of the course of study.

The subtler aspects of learning method have to do with the detailed individuality of the learner himself. Just as introductory precepts may wash over the stunned mind of a fresher, so, at any time, the learner's personal situation may isolate him from what may seem the glib precepts of common-sense. Rules of study may have a hard struggle with the pangs of love, or a reputation in the tutor's study with a different kind of reputation in the ballroom and bar, or the deeply ingrained habits and expectations of home with a different set of habits and expectations in college. Each individual's concept of himself, expressed in personal style and in characteristic modes of psychological self-defence, has been built up over long and critical periods and shapes responses in the learning situation. These styles and defences include diverse manifestations from extreme earnestness to *je m'en foutisme*, from cynicism to naïvety, from diffidence to conceit, from practical realism to wild escapism (or escapadism), from studious withdrawal to boisterous social commitment. The sharp definition of learning precepts becomes blurred under the influence of such individual variety—variety of situation and variety of intrinsic personality. Indeed, it is often said that an important part of higher learning (as of all learning) consists in learning from this variety of people and situations—learning how to cope with life's ordinary social situations as well as with its more specifically academic and intellectual ones.

Variability in learning and the developmental approach

All that has been said hitherto might be regarded as a very rough sketch map of student learning in colleges and universities, with five major areas marked off on the map— the learners themselves, the things they are learning, their academic institutions, the teaching methods used, and the learners' own techniques and styles of learning. These represent a complex set of phenomena, and it is clear that each individual area is itself subdivided into a tremendous variety and complexity, only briefly suggested in the foregoing analysis. Not only are the relevant variables of learning very numerous, but also the means of assessing them do not have a high degree of precision, although one can see that there is liable to be a wide variation among individuals on any single variable. The fact of variability among individuals and, indeed, among different occasions for the same individual, is one of the most striking features of learning, whether complex or simple. Much study of learning is an attempt to determine what governs this variability, and to do so in as reliably quantitative terms as can be established, despite the difficulties of measuring human performance with accuracy and reliability. Those who have aspired to the greatest quantitative precision have tended to study the learning of animals or extremely elementary forms of human learning. At the same time, the study of complex learning has not stood still but surpasses considerably the 'common-sense' opinions and practices of those who pay little attention to it. For example, although the analysis of higher learning just presented is intended only as a broad survey, many of the factors mentioned are continually ignored in the practices and opinions of otherwise sophisticated teachers and students.

Again, although the concept of variability may seem very simple and obvious, experienced teachers constantly demonstrate their lack of detailed appreciation of it, so that they detect significance in small arbitrary differences (say between 64 and 66 per cent) in examination marks, or imagine that there is something more than conventional convenience in calling a pass-mark forty or fifty or any other number. And, of course, when one must handle human variability in several dimensions, oversimplified interpretations abound as in the enthusiasm of the nineteen-thirties and -forties for the idea of stable individual

14

'intelligence'—an enthusiasm perhaps only matched by the naïvety of the sixties in trying to represent 'intelligence' as a manufacturable commodity.

Whatever the difficulty of coping with complexity it is the only way to understanding learning, and one must, as a beginning, try to list the kinds of evidence and the areas of special enquiry that are required or suggested by the 'common-sense' account of complex learning given in this chapter. Perhaps the first and most obvious need is to consider learning phenomena in relation to human chronological development, for so much of individual learning is shaped by previous learning. For this reason, the next chapter makes a new beginning—a developmental one— and is followed by others which deal with learning during the periods of primary and secondary schooling respectively. This will provide a fuller range of reference for discussing particular aspects of learning. Even were one to pursue particular problems of student learning, it would be difficult to do so without referring to evidence that derives from earlier developmental or educational stages. In following this pattern of analysis it should be possible to illustrate more fully the significance, already stressed, of variability. It should be possible to see how the learning problems of more advanced stages are partly the product of learning experiences at earlier stages, and how learning problems and solutions are defined by human individuality, educational curricula, the character of scholastic and non-scholastic institutions, teaching methods, and learning methods. What theories can one expect to encounter and what kinds of evidence?

Five kinds of evidence

Without going into details, refinements, or controversies, one should mention five major kinds of approach or evidence—the behaviourist, the configurationist, the psychoanalytical, the sociological, and the *ad hoc* empirical. The behaviourist approach thinks of itself as being the most scientific. It is concerned to eliminate from its field of study anything that is not manifest in some form of observable behaviour, including verbal behaviour. It is concerned with what is observable and quantifiable and with attempting to subsume findings under some systematic theory. If the individual has private experiences which *never* manifest themselves in any observable way, then these are outside the realm of scientific study and cannot explain anything. In their eagerness for scientific precision and system behaviourists have tended to concentrate on situations which favour these and, therefore, have accumulated more solid evidence about such situations and less (although still a certain amount) about complex human phenomena. The strength of behaviourism is its striving to satisfy scientific criteria of evidence, its weakness, the tendency to overlook phenomena which do not lend themselves to its kind of experimentation and sometimes to fall into logical errors from which a more sympathetic appreciation of philosophy might have saved it. The typical evidence of behaviourists is carefully controlled experiments on animal learning.

Animal learning experiments are not, of course, a sufficient sign of behaviourism in the above sense. The gestalt or configurationist school of psychology has a tradition of animal study with a different emphasis. The emphasis is, briefly, on the significance of insight into the structure of a learning situation as an important feature of learning, as distinct from behaviourist accounts which have no use for unobservable 'mentalistic' concepts such as 'insight'. Whether or not such concepts are necessary for a complete explanation, they tend to persist, partly because human beings often feel that they do have something that one might call 'insight' into situations, and partly because even animal learning seems reluctant to succumb completely to an entirely mechanical kind of explanation. The white rats in their mazes sometimes behave *as if* they had insight.

Various psychoanalytic approaches to learning occupy almost the converse role to that of behaviourism. Here there has been much less concern for scientific accuracy or control, but many attempts to supply psychoanalytic interpretations of even complex human phenomena. Typically a psychoanalytical explanation would emphasize the persisting and widespread influence of two things—the infant's earliest experiences of human relationship, particularly with the mother, and, deriving from these first emotional experiences, the liability of any person's behaviour to exemplify significant patterns which the person himself does not notice, or to which he gives a different interpretation from what a detached but understanding observer would give. This is reified in the myth of the unconscious—the notion of a kind of subterranean psychological realm which operates on one's behaviour without oneself realizing how, in detail, it does. On this account, a student's conception of himself, and his characteristic modes of unconsciously preserving this conception against the deflationary attacks of the world and other people, would be considered to stem from his earliest affective relationships in the family. Although the earlier psychoanalytic mythologies have been severely criticized for being unscientific, and even ordinary psychoanalytical terms criticized for their ambiguous meanings, more recent writers have pruned the mythology and ambiguity, and brought psychoanalytic ideas into closer accord with ordinary biological and social analysis of human behaviour. They have also attempted to make statistically controlled comparisons of the effects of different experiences in infancy on subsequent personality characteristics. Much evidence in the psychoanalytical area derives from clinical observation of individuals or groups, with a resulting strength in interesting and plausible detail but the accompanying weakness of variable interpretation and the fallibility of human judgement.

The fourth approach to learning is associated with the study of social psychology and sociology. The two studies can best be viewed as overlapping one another. Social psychology is concerned with the influence of social factors on individual behaviour. Sociology is concerned with social relations in themselves, and particularly with the operations and interrelations of social institutions such as family, school, college, trade union, industry, bureaucracy, or profession. Social psychology reminds one that social influences operate on all learning situations and that an analysis of learning is not likely to be complete if it thinks of the learner as a kind of detached individual in a social void. Sociology reminds one that each individual finds himself with a role, or several roles, in a social institution, or several institutions. Whether the individual is a new baby in a family or a parent with roles outside as well as inside the family, these roles create complex patterns of expectation to which their occupants tend to conform. Roles may also create conflicts which have to be resolved, just as the university undergraduate may have to opt for the union presidency with *its* set of expectancies or for a first-class degree with its different expectancies, or another may have to reconcile the low educational expectancies of a less educated home with the high expectancies of a school or college. The evidence of sociology derives from the close study of the many actual institutions of society and of the ways in which they influence one another and the individuals belonging to them.

The fifth approach to learning is that of *ad hoc* study of specific learning problems, often by means of matching groups in as many relevant respects as possible (age, sex, family background, previous education, etc.) and then comparing statistically their performances in respect of two different learning or teaching methods which one wants to compare. This method of matched groups has been used to study programmed learning, aids to reading, memorization techniques, methods of infant-teaching, and many other educational performances. When the matched-groups technique is not adequate for the circumstances it is sometimes possible to use various statistical techniques to determine how a complex series of factors contribute to a particular phenomenon. Such techniques have given us, among other things, a much better understanding of how educational achievement is shaped by various social factors, of how patterns of test results may be analysed, and of how the infinite variety of human personality may be related (not reduced) to a smaller number of explanatory hypotheses. Direct empirical assaults on specific learning problems may be useful or necessary for giving one a valid pointer to specific and speedy action or decision. They also discipline one to analyse relevant factors in more detail, and in more quantitative terms, than customary 'common-sense' does. Their shortcoming is that, by their nature, they may be limited by a particular set of circumstances (the schools of one area, the educational conventions of one country) and fail to achieve as much generality of conclusion as some learning theorists would like to have.

It may be useful to recognize certain provisos about the study of learning so that they do not later act like red herrings across the main arguments. One is that there is no single theory of learning that is universally accepted and that neatly subsumes all learning phenomena : learning is a controversial topic. A second is that many modern generalizations about learning can be matched in the writings of past centuries; but, commonly, the wisdom of the past in such matters was expressed in less specific terms, was lacking in quantitative reference points, was less closely related to theories which themselves had undergone quantitative assessment, and was admitted and acted on by exceptional educators rather than by the typical educator. It demands intellectual discrimination to avoid the deplorable contempt for the past that characterizes some writings in psychology and the equally deplorable obscurantism of some traditionalists (to give them a kind name) who ignore the criteria mentioned in the last sentence. A third proviso is that there is no justification for assuming that the analysis of learning should ever be strikingly simple or non-technical, although one might in practice strive for simplicity. Where many variables operate complexly together and where an appreciation of their statistical patterns of variation and relationship is indispensable, one must expect that, even among educated people, some will prefer to ignore what they have not seriously applied themselves to understanding.

It would be a large historical endeavour to relate changing analyses of learning to changing patterns of education in schools, colleges, and society. One may, however, suggest that the growing implementation of individual and small-group methods of learning, the movements for curricular change, the increased concern with the individual and his family in addition to the subject of study and its scholastic setting, the abandonment of corporal punishment as a standard sanction for learning, the refinement of ideas about how one kind of learning may transfer to another learning situation, the relegation of rote learning to a subordinate place in the scheme of things, the concern to relate different stages of learning to one another, and the greater technical care taken in assessing people for educational purposes are examples of changes which most people would judge were for the better and which have owed not only their inspiration but their modes of implementation to modern analytic approaches to learning.

2

Pre-school learning

Three approaches to infant learning

'At first the infant, mewling and puking in the nurse's arms . . .'—what and how does *he* learn? What activities of his produce a relatively permanent effect on later activities? What knowledge, understanding, or skill does he obtain by study, instruction, or experience? A mother thinking of her own children may doubt whether one can generalize in view of the differences among the children even of one family. And any one struck by the quite rapid change from week to week—later, month to month—in a young infant may wonder how one can analyse such a rapid, and often wayward, process. And yet people have recognized in widely separated historical periods the fact of infant impressionability—the fact that what happens in the first years of life has particular power and significance for later development and learning.

The psychological approaches mentioned in the preceding chapter lead to particular interpretations of infancy and, commonly, to an emphasis on its importance as a basis for later development to a complete adulthood. The behaviourist is interested in analysing quantitatively how particular infant responses and patterns of response are reinforced or extinguished or shaped into more complex patterns of behaviour. The psychoanalyst has his own descriptive clinical language for describing the aspects of

21

infant experience that he wishes to relate to subsequent adult patterns. The sociologist charts the influence of social class and home background on patterns of child-rearing. The *ad hoc* experimentalist studies the development of language and perception, the effects of different kinds of nursery or other prescholastic education, and any other specific problems that become interesting and are susceptible of systematic study. Of course, these approaches are not equally distinct from one another. They are a simplification of a very much greater variety of interpretations, some of which overlap extensively, others of which tend to be distinct and deadly enemies (some behaviourists and some psychoanalysts, for example). The present chapter, after a brief reference to the topic of nature and nurture, will give examples of behaviourist, psychoanalytic, and sociological approaches to infant learning, and conclude with some general comments on these viewed all together in relation to learning.

Nature and nurture

Since all learning is influenced by earlier learning it would be interesting to put one's finger on a child's very first learning—to get to the source of the complex stream that develops so rapidly even in the first year of life. One might then see what is the embryonic nature of human learning. Earlier generations of psychologists attempted to do this by distinguishing what seemed to be hereditary from what seemed to be environmental influences, and by distinguishing behaviour that could be produced by training from behaviour that seemed to depend on an appropriate degree of maturation rather than training. The first line of enquiry produced many studies of how children with different degrees of shared genetical inheritance (identical twins, fraternal or non-identical twins, ordinary brothers and sisters, unrelated children) varied in intellectual and other

22

characteristics according to different kinds of upbringing (maternal home, foster home, orphanage). For example, if identical twins reared apart from one another still resemble one another psychologically more than do brothers and sisters of one family (siblings) reared together, then this would suggest that the identical heredity of the twins accounts for the difference. One might think of it as a competition to see which group can end up most like one another. The twins being more environmentally separated, have to count on their genetical identity, whereas the control group of ordinary siblings, being genetically similar but not identical, have to count more on a common environment. Holzinger found in one study that the intelligence quotients of pairs of fraternal twins reared together correlated within pairs to the extent of 0.63 whereas the corresponding correlation for identical twins reared apart was 0.76 (Newman, Freeman, Holzinger, 1937). A common environment was associated with considerable intellectual similarity, but an identical heredity with rather more.

Another variant of the first line of enquiry was to compare equivalent groups of children brought up in comparable circumstances, except that one group were brought up by their natural parents while the other were brought up by foster parents. Burks and Leahy found that the correlation between the intelligence quotients of foster-children and foster-parents did not exceed 0.2, whereas the corresponding correlation for children and their natural parents was nearer 0.5 (Newman, 1937). This suggested that differential heredity limited the powers of a common environment to make children resemble foster-parents intellectually, although a common environment was associated with at least some degree of common learning as reflected in the correlation of 0.2.

The second line of enquiry consisted in comparing the learning of simple tasks (buttoning, cutting with scissors, stair-climbing, tricycling, swimming) by twins, one of

23

whom received no special training, the other of whom was coached in the activity. If learning mattered as well as maturation, the twin who was trained should have performed better and sooner than his untrained fellow twin. In some tasks this was found to be the case, but it was also found in some such studies that, when the untrained twin got the chance of learning the performance at a later date, he learned it quite effectively in a shorter period of time. Such studies left one with the sense that some infant learning could be accelerated up to a point by means of training, but that maturation would do the trick equally well at a slightly later stage. Some psychologists then tended to support an educational policy of relative non-interference in infancy. Children were simply to be allowed to develop naturally in accordance with the maturational pattern of human life. Since many educationists and psychologists now advocate a much more 'interfering' policy, one is bound to ask what has produced such a radical change. Fowler points out that maturation-versus-training experiments tended to ignore the fact that the untrained control child would still be exposed to general training influences in the environment, even if he was not trained in the specific experimental task (Staats, 1964). But this is a minor objection compared with the extent of the change in attitude that has occurred.

One vivid statement of the modern reaction against the concepts of so-called 'fixed intelligence' and 'predetermined development' can be read in the second and third chapters of J. M. Hunt's *Intelligence and Experience* (Hunt, 1961), but some expression of hostility to the nature-nurture controversy of the thirties and forties is almost *de rigueur* in modern environmentalist accounts of human behaviour, as in Lipsitt's comment that 'the nature-nurture conflict . . . is widely recognized as substantially empty' (Stevenson, 1967, p. 225). Genetical factors are obviously one of the major determinants of what an individual may become, but we cannot do much about them. Environmental factors, on the other hand, are both influential and, in principle, controllable. It is more profitable, therefore, to study environmental shaping of behaviour with a view to producing behaviour that is more useful for whatever purposes we set ourselves. This, of course, was well recognized intellectually by at least some of the last generation of psychologists, but their successors seem to have identified themselves more passionately with an environmentalist emphasis.

This emphasis has grown as fresh evidence has appeared about how the environment shapes the earliest learning and as fresh holes have been picked in some (not all) of the evidence of earlier times. It has always been recognized that there are practical difficulties about collecting evidence based on twins. There are difficulties of finding a sufficient number of them and of ensuring that their upbringings conform with the patterns necessary to constitute a decisive test. Hunt (1961) points out that twins may be reared apart and yet be in virtually the same environment, in so far as the environments are characterized by uniform child-rearing practices prevalent in a particular culture. Mussen (1965, p. 42) warns of a danger in the opposite direction—that children reared in the same home may be assumed to have the same environment, when, in fact, there are important, if subtle, psychological differences for various siblings (being youngest or oldest, prettiest or ugliest, mother's favourite or father's despair, etc.). Then there are problems about assessing the psychological traits that have been typically studied in the nature-nurture controversy. A person's intelligence quotient may vary from one test to another, or from one time to another, and is itself a complex product of assumed genetic factors together with learning experiences, current motivation, and a particular culture's choice of test problems. These are some of the considerations that have accompanied the

25

environmentalist trend. A large problem is still left over for the environmentalist. He has burst some of the bonds of genetic fatalism and demonstrated many of the modes of environmental shaping, but he is only on the threshold of knowledge about how to undo the detrimental shaping of certain social environments and substitute the beneficial shaping that educationally fortunate children receive from sympathetic and encouraging homes.

There is now a subtler appreciation of the complex operations of environment and heredity. With a difficult psychological trait, such as intelligence, in which heredity and environment are fused, one can admit a genetic component without being able to give a precise genetical specification of it. At the other extreme, there are some conditions of psychological interest, such as whether one is a man or woman, which have precisely known genetic features. Whether or not the genetical basis of any human phenomenon is understood in detail, the phenomenon itself is a product of genetical and environmental factors. Moreover, the final significance of this genetic-environmental product depends on how a particular society evaluates it. The brilliant scientist requires a society that esteems scientific brilliance, the beauty queen a society which chooses to hold beauty competitions. Environmental factors themselves may grossly or subtly predispose an infant in certain directions, even while he is still a foetus in the womb. The mother's age, emotional state, attitudes, nutrition, and health influence directly or indirectly the baby's delivery into the world and his capacity to develop once he is born. Growth is continuous from foetus to new-born child. Genetic and environmental factors tend to confirm one another. But, if certain limiting conditions of learning are being set before a child is even born, the term *learning* is hardly appropriate until he is born, and, therefore, one turns again to the question of what is the earliest learning and how it takes place.

Behaviourist approaches

It may be helpful to begin by stating briefly some of the essential concepts of behaviouristic analysis. Firstly, as already mentioned at the end of the first chapter, the behaviourist concerns himself only with overt behaviour, with behaviour that can be measured objectively in some way. It may be that people have private experiences that are never, or never fully, expressed in any way, but then, by that very fact, no one else can know about them. If these experiences are ever made known to anyone in any form, then they become at least partly overt and, therefore, in principle, susceptible of objective study. Second, such overt behaviour is regarded as a set of responses to some set of stimuli, arising inside or outside the person's body. We know that our brains are physiologically stimulated by the impulses arriving from the various organs of sense. Other impulses go out from the brain along the nervous system to the muscles involved in the various movements of the body, including the movements of speech. The behaviourist would account for all human behaviour in terms of such patterns of stimulus and response, and in terms of the intervening physiological operations of the brain. Although we do not, in fact, know enough about the brain to give a complete explanation along these lines, we know more than we once did. This way of looking at behaviour is at least susceptible of scientific study and explanation, whereas accounts in terms of private experience ('My feelings made me do it', 'I did it from intuition', etc.) are alleged to be untestable and, therefore, without explanatory force.

Third, proceeding from this stimulus-brain-response model of behaviour, the behaviourist makes great use of the idea of conditioning. In its classical form (Pavlovian conditioning) this is the process whereby a natural or unconditioned stimulus-response connection (e.g., a dog's salivating in response to the presentation of food) is modified so that some new or conditioned stimulus (e.g., the sound of a buzzer) also evokes the salivating response. In another kind of conditioning (operant conditioning) any response at all that an organism makes can be made more likely to happen again (reinforced) by an appropriate form of reward, or made less likely to happen again (extinguished) by withholding reward. By manipulating appropriate forms of reinforcement over a sufficient length of time, one could shape quite complex behaviour, let us say in a child, without the child realizing that one was doing so. One would begin by reinforcing (perhaps with sweets or words of approbation) all behaviour that was roughly in the intended direction, and then gradually refine the programme so that only the precise behaviour required was reinforced. Responses that conflicted with the desired pattern of behaviour would be extinguished by going unrewarded. This, at least, is the general principle of conditioning: the practice is obviously a more difficult question. With human beings one is rarely the sole controller of the reinforcement situation, and the home, for example, may be powerfully reinforcing the very items of behaviour that the school is trying to extinguish, and vice versa.

The preceding paragraphs are just an introductory glossary to certain key terms in behaviourist analysis. They should facilitate the understanding of the rest of this section, but they do not do justice to behaviourism itself, which is a large field requiring study in its own right. Some may find the rather mechanical model of human behaviour repugnant in itself, but this would not be a reasoned argument against behaviourism if the model constituted a satisfactory explanation. Moreover, modern behaviourists have advanced considerably over earlier generations in their attention to the subtler aspects of behaviour, and particularly verbal behaviour. Some may find

28

behaviouristic analysis too alien from the psychological conceptions of 'common-sense', or too lacking in reference to the very aspects of personal experience that one would like to see psychologically explained. This may be only hesitation in the face of unfamiliar concepts, but it may also be the spotting of some genuine limitation in behaviourist concepts, a sense that the behaviourist is trying to force us to accept his definition of what psychology is to mean. Then some may feel that the behaviourist is guilty of philosophic confusion. They might argue, as suggested in the earliest paragraphs of this book, that conditioning is not the same as learning, that stimulus-response behaviour is not the same as human action, that no amount of physiological explanation could be exhaustive as a psychological explanation—in fact, that being a person means more than being an organism. Even if any such objections are felt to be valid, it is worth while exploring how far one can go along the behaviourist way, and the following are some examples of behaviourist approaches to infant learning.

William Kessen reports on the sucking and looking responses of about two dozen infants observed at the Yale-New Haven Hospital during their first four days of life (Stevenson, 1967). Some were good suckers, some poor suckers, and the good suckers were more readily quietened than the poor by presentation of a nipple. Moreover, sucking appeared to reduce the amount of infant movement independently of the experience of being fed. In fact, there appeared to be a congenital association between sucking and general movement, for it could not be linked with other variables, such as sex or weight, that were considered. Studies of looking ('ocular orientation') by newborn babies showed a greater concentration of looks or orientations on the vertices of a triangle that was presented before them than on a homogeneous black field of vision, suggesting that the act of looking is in some degree

29

organized at birth, and possibly supporting the idea that the infant begins to construct his perceptual world from birth. Kessen suggests that development does not depend *only* on 'the repair of physiological deficit' (feeding the hungry baby, for example) or on 'social reinforcement' (making him feel what a good baby he is). The baby positively constructs his world, his own first notion of reality. 'Adult reality is the last of a long series of theories of reality that the child develops, modifies, and sometimes rejects' (Stevenson, p. 150).

An essay by R. L. Fantz, published along with Kessen's contrasts the view of learning that defines it in terms of response tendencies with an alternative view that learning may include 'the acquisition of knowledge apart from specific changes in response' (Stevenson, p. 182). Infants, even before they are two weeks old, have been shown to give more attention to a complex pattern than to a plain grey surface. As they grow older various other specific patterns seem to command more attention. Fantz suggests that such small temporary changes in response may contribute to longer-term behavioural change, and that human beings can, in any case, take in information without manifest behavioural response. One may read a book and 'learn' a great deal from it and yet observers may neither know that one has read the book nor, if they do, be able to link the reading of the book with any new behaviour. One might counter-argue that they could discover the links, given sufficient time and facilities, but Fantz is presumably making the point that there would always be a residue of private knowledge which had not been expressed in overt behaviour but which nonetheless existed.

Hanuš Papoušek studied simple behaviour changes, induced by a conditioning procedure, in newborn infants, three-month-old infants, and five-month-old infants. The babies would turn their head left or right to the natural stimulus of milk from a bottle (unconditioned stimulus).

By repeatedly sounding a bell or buzzer just before the offer of milk the head-turning response came to be elicited by the stimulus of the bell or buzzer (conditioned stimulus). Further experiments showed that the conditioned response could be extinguished and restored, that the infants could be taught to discriminate between bell and buzzer, and that the discriminatory responses could be reversed so that the response to bell was transferred to buzzer, and vice versa. The number in each experimental group was about 14 to 16, and great care appears to have been taken to safeguard both the babies as babies and the experimental conditions as requisites for valid inference.

One of the interesting aspects of this study is its precise illustration of individual variation in learning (or at least, conditionability) at these early ages—both variation within each age group and, of course, between age groups. At about three weeks of age the average *number of trials* necessary to reach the specified criterion of head-turning was 177, with wide variation among individuals. This number dropped to 42 for the three-month-olds and 28 for the five-month-olds, with a great drop too in variability within age-groups. The average *time taken* to respond after the appropriate sound (response latency) dropped from 4·95 seconds to 3·92 seconds, and then to 3·55 seconds for the oldest infants, but the variability for this measure increased within groups from younger to older. During the first three months of life this kind of conditioning seems to be slow and unstable. The youngest group averaged two and a half months before they could respond discriminatively to bell or buzzer. Some would not use the word 'learning' for this kind of induction of behavioural change, but it certainly shows some interesting aspects of behavioural modifiability at an early age and throws at least one ray of light on early 'learning' in a broad sense.

The Papoušek study illustrates behavioural change

through traditional conditioning, in which a natural, or unlearned, response to an unconditioned stimulus (e.g. a baby sucking a teat) is transferred (with some modifications) to a conditioned stimulus (e.g. a bell or buzzer). Other studies have shown how, by operant conditioning, any response can be reinforced so that it tends to occur more often or more strongly. For example, Salzinger and others report how operant conditioning was used to produce changes in the speech behaviour of children between five and seven (Staats, 1964, p. 90). The children were invited to play the game of trying to make a papier-mâché clown happy by talking to him. There was a red light bulb in the clown's nose and the experimenters were able to switch it on when certain predetermined speech responses by the children took place. The lighting-up of the clown's nose was a kind of reward, reinforcing only those speech responses which the experimenters chose to reinforce. By such reinforcement they were able to induce a faster rate of speech, and also the more frequent use of first personal pronouns, among the children. There was another group of children, used as an experimental control, whose behaviour received no reinforcement—no illuminated nose for them! The only change in their speech towards the clown was that it gradually diminished in quantity (experimentally extinguished) as they received no reinforcement.

Those who approach learning from the angle of conditioning have extended the kind of argument and evidence just illustrated to all human behaviour at all ages. If a baby's reactions can be reinforced, extinguished, or variously patterned by means of a nipple, or a five-year-old's with an illuminated clown's nose, so, it is argued, can children's or adults' behaviour or attitudes be shaped by material and social reinforcement. It has been experimentally demonstrated that adult speech patterns can be shaped by an experimenter doing as little as muttering 'Mh'm' after certain utterances and doing nothing after others. Thus a stimulus ('Mh'm') which has no natural response-evoking power comparable with the power of suckable objects to evoke a baby's sucking, acquires such power, presumably from its association with the social approval which human beings have learned to need. 'Mh'm' is a conditioned reinforcing stimulus, powered by the social significance of the expression, evoking a particular attitude response when it is uttered.

Staats, in an interesting study of how speech behaviour develops as compared with reading behaviour, points out how poor readers are typically deprived of all the strong reinforcers which would normally lead to better reading (Staats, 1964, pp. 67-81). Speech behaviour is reinforced by the strong reinforcers of parental approval, material rewards, and the sheer achievement of the child hearing himself. Moreover, this process occurs over a prolonged period and each reinforcement is individually applied to the particular child. Reading, by contrast, is often presented as an intensive group task concentrated into specific periods. This gives an aversive or discouraging effect to all the stimuli associated with the reading situation, while evasive behaviour (talking, playing, daydreaming) is strengthened. Staats suggests that reading programmes should be strongly gradualist rather than intensive, that all social reinforcers should be fully employed, and that material reinforcers, in the shape of toys, snacks, and the like, should be tried where social reinforcement is at its weakest—for example, presumably, in children whose homes are outstandingly marked by educational and social disadvantage. Staats's analysis illustrates how behaviourist principles can be applied to the perennial early learning problem of learning to read. It reminds one of the power of social reinforcement—at every step encouraging and improving the fortunate child while discouraging and impeding the socially unfortunate—and it recognizes the need to go back to material reinforcers as a first step towards creating social reinforcers where these have not already been established. The old-fashioned schoolmistress with a bag of sweets in her handbag perhaps never realized how psychologically advanced she was.

Many children of pre-school age are fortunate in that their families come near to observing the best behaviourist principles, even if they do not recognize this fact. The children's behaviour is gradually and gently shaped by reinforcing certain items and not reinforcing others. Material rewards and social approval, or, on the negative side, the withholding of these, guide the child relatively painlessly into the acquisition of appropriate skills and attitudes. Such children sometimes acquire the initial reading skills before going to school just as readily as they acquire the initial speaking skills, for they are not presented with the talking/reading discrepancy analysed by Staats. University graduates, reflecting upon their own education, quite often say: 'I don't remember learning to read. My mother used to read me stories and talk about them. There were lots of children's books about the house. I didn't have to learn to read at school.' These are the fortunate children; but there are as many or more whose homes do not provide such an agreeable grounding. In their case a quite different set of behaviours may be reinforced and, in many areas of desirable pre-school development, there may be no stimulus to any kind of behaviour. Reading, for example, may be actively repudiated as an irrelevant activity, or simply neglected because it has not entered into the particular family or neighbourhood culture. Material rewards may be few for any of the family. Social rewards may be distributed on different principles from those prevailing in the school-orientated classes of society.

Some behaviourist thinkers have attempted to apply their own psychological analyses to the practical problems of educationally or socially handicapped pre-school children. They have argued that what happens naturally for the fortunate must be systematically contrived for the less fortunate. 'Cultural discontinuities' or 'socio-cognitive dissonance' between home and school must be narrowed by means of sustained, well-financed, validly organized pre-school programmes. What counts as valid must be found out in practice, but it would be expected to include (i) supplementing the meagre educational resources of certain homes, (ii) familiarizing children with things, ideas, and activities that they would have encountered in a more favoured home, (iii) countering any positively pernicious effects of a bad environment, and (iv) evolving an 'adult-support' programme—which means winning over parents to support the efforts for the children and supporting the parents themselves in attitudes which may be new within their social world. All of this may sound fairly obvious, despite the fact that communities have failed to apply it, but what is perhaps more particular about the behaviourist approach to the problem is the elaboration of practical details on the basis of a systematic psychological analysis.

One of the most important points is the emphasis on sustained educational stimulation (of the right kind) and systematic control of the most powerful reinforcing agents (particularly, the mother's sympathy and understanding for the programme). The most severely culturally deprived children particularly need to learn how to use verbal labels as a first step in learning how to think. This means that the special educational environment provided should constantly stimulate them to use more words and to use them with increasing precision and discrimination on the basis of direct experience of what the words refer to. This process is so automatic in a favourable cultural environment that teachers have had to learn to analyse what is sometimes taken for granted and to construct detailed programmes of elementary experience and learning for children whose homes do not have such programmes built

35

into their human fabric. Carl Bereiter and others in an essay on 'An Academically Oriented Pre-School for Culturally Deprived Children' discuss this approach in some detail (Hechinger, 1966, pp. 105-35). The emphasis on a direct instructional attack, reflected in the essay's title, is interesting after the relative non-interference philosophy of recent decades.

Martin Deutsch, in the same volume, goes so far as to say that 'the overgeneralized influence on some sections of early childhood education of the emphasis in the child guidance movement upon protecting the child from stress, creating a supportive environment, and resolving emotional conflicts, has done more to misdirect and retard the fields of child care, guidance, and development than any other single influence' (Hechinger, 1966, p. 92). One might, of course, want to underline the words 'overgeneralized' and 'some', at the beginning of Deutsch's remark, to keep it in proper perspective. Nevertheless, it is impressive that a refined version of traditional direct-instruction approaches to learning should be so vigorously defended after half a century or more of what has been called 'soft pedagogy'. It is to be hoped that the *laudatores temporis acti* will observe that this new 'hard pedagogy' is a refined, not a crude, version of hammering in the learning for the good of their young souls. J. M. Hunt takes a moderately optimistic view of the possibility of reversing 'experiential deprivation during infancy' (Hechinger, 1966, p. 54), but the general observation of educational and social processes does not suggest that it will be always, or even often, easy to bring about the arrangements which pre-school compensatory education assumes to be necessary for success.

Psychoanalytic approaches

The intention of the preceding section was to look at some aspects of early learning through behaviourist eyes. The emphasis was on overt and preferably measurable items of behaviour rather than on subjective experience; on evolving specific detailed techniques for shaping specific behavioural responses rather than on general advice about general or indefinite patterns of behaviour; and on linking educational programmes as nearly as possible with psycological analyses that are thought to have been well validated by observation and experiment. Even where the behaviourist may seem to fall short of his ideal in practice, he does not abandon it. He has definite ideas about the most effective approaches to learning, even if he may have to take some leaps in the dark, like one of his own white rats, to span the gulfs between strict experimental evidence and the practical organization of complex human learning. Psychoanalytic approaches to learning have been as widely influential as behaviourism (perhaps more so), but they have arisen from clinical study rather than experiment, they have often been rather general and imprecise in their evidence and in their conceptual analysis, and they have sometimes given rise to a degree of speculative elaboration which has invited the sharp criticism especially of those not committed to a psychoanalytic point of view. Just as the earlier discussion of behaviourism has been cavalier in ignoring important variations and refinements, so the following account of psychoanalysis is intended to draw attention only to some of the major points relevant to the present discussion of learning.

For psychoanalysis, the baby's physical, social, and emotional relationship with the mother, and subsequently with the rest of his family, is of fundamental importance. The experiences of satisfaction or frustration, tension or relaxation, harmony or conflict, intolerance or tolerance, that the infant experiences in his first years will generate characteristic patterns of behaviour which will tend to spread into later life and into situations which are, on the surface, radically different from those of the infant in

37

arms. The infant is not just a physical organism that requires appropriate physical nourishment; he is, from birth, a psychological being, slowly developing a sense of just who he is and by what means he will assert and protect himself. If he is able to trust his mother and family this will be demonstrated in 'the ease of his feeding, the depth of his sleep, the relaxation of his bowels' (Erikson, 1965, p. 239) when he is an infant, and will be manifest in his self-confidence and social ease in later years. Correspondingly, any lack of steady affection and security will disturb the infant's early experience of feeding, sleeping, and excreting, and such disturbances will spread to later activities, producing perhaps hesitation, conflict, or other impediments in the course of growing to adulthood. The difficult feeder in infancy, the food-fad in adult life, are expressing psychological, not just physical, dissatisfaction. Even 'ordinary' people are put off their meals—or, alternatively, driven to excessive drinking and eating—by psychological upsets. Similarly, a child who experiences intense and early bowel-training may, in the view of some, develop a constrained and rigid kind of personality as an adult.

A second major point is that internal psychological conflict is a feature of human development from earliest infancy. This conflict is not just a question of the disparity between understandable longings and equally understandable limitations of the social world in satisfying them. It is not, that is, only a question of baby wanting all of the mother's attention when he must in fact share it with father, and the other children. It is a conflict that is developed irrationally by the infant's assumed fantasies about life. Just as adults sometimes intensify or alleviate their own internal conflicts by day-dreaming themselves into an unrealistic sense of power or hostility or some such feeling, so, it is claimed, the infant develops fantasies, particularly about his mother or father. He may have an oral fantasy of eating his mother up (an idea, incidentally, that enters into the baby-talk of adult lovers—'I could eat you up!'), and yet also feel intensely guilty and afraid that his cannibalism will incur fearful retribution. He may want later to 'marry' his mother but fear paternal reprisals. The point is that irrational fantasies are an important ingredient of psychological development and one can only fully understand development by studying such irrationality. Much psychoanalytic writing has been concerned with the detailed analysis of such phenomena, which are here only briefly mentioned.

A third major feature of psychoanalysis is its account of the various ways in which individuals learn unconsciously to protect themselves psychologically. 'Every conscience,' in Erikson's words, 'whether in an individual or a group, has not only specific contents but also its own particular logic which safeguards its coherence' (Erikson, 1965, p. 124). One might say, not just every conscience, but every consciousness. The individual *rationalizes*, giving reasons for his behaviour or attitude which satisfy him but perhaps not an independent observer. He *projects* on to others the blame for behaviour or attitudes which are, to others, conspicuous in himself. He *daydreams* himself into triumphs and preferments which others do not see him attaining. He *represses* (that is, becomes unaware of) ideas that others, nevertheless, see to be influential in his behaviour and which sometimes give themselves away in oddities of conduct or in slips of the tongue ('It's not that I like him—I mean, dislike him'). He *regresses* to an earlier stage of development and has an infantile temper tantrum or seeks to be babied. These are a few of the specific modes of unconscious protective adaptation.

While any one person may illustrate any of these mechanisms from time to time, one or two such psychological defences may be particularly characteristic of his whole way of life. He may defend his conception of himself by an easy natural friendliness in all relations, or by a wary

39

suspicion of people and their doings, or by a blustering bonhomie, or by a careful delimitation of his life to a safe familiar setting. The predominant character of such psychological defence-works may vary widely from person to person, and, any one pattern of defence may be extensively elaborated, depending on how susceptible to attack it is felt to be. Although such defences may strike one by their weirdness only in exceptional cases, it would be maintained, on this view, that everyone does have such defences to bolster up his conception of himself and his assumed role in society. Such defences go beyond the minimum ratiocination demanded by immediate objective circumstances and derive some of their strength or compulsiveness from the earliest experiences of infancy. There must be defences, in this sense, for each individual must have some sense of definite identity—he must construct and defend a particular notion of who he is or is going to be. Otherwise he goes to pieces, as the everyday saying accurately expresses it. What matters to the psychoanalyst, as to the student of people as learners, is that an individual's self-concept should not be highly disparate with objective realities, for such a discrepancy too can lead to the collapse of the person's morale.

The mother-child relationship, the prevalence of fantasy and internal psychological conflict from early infancy onwards, the building up of a self-concept and various defences for it, the influence of the earliest experiences in these matters on later behaviour and attitudes, the individual's unconsciousness of how, in detail, such factors shape his life even if he is conscious that they *are* shaping it—these are some of the most important points of the psychoanalytic approach, which invites us to distrust current appearances and search for underlying realities in infancy—'Our Adult World and Its Roots in Infancy', as Melanie Klein's pamphlet has it (Klein, 1959). There are two obvious implications for learning. The first is that the most important early learning is the unconscious learning (if the phrase does not contradict itself—which some might argue it does) that takes place in the ways just outlined. It is most important because it is associated with the basic bodily processes that almost dominate infancy and that are very important even for adults whom they do not happen to dominate. And it is important because of the spread of fundamental attitudinal reactions from these bodily experiences to other aspects of life.

The second implication for learning derives from the first. It is that items of general social or scholastic learning which have often been, and still are sometimes, thought of as more or less *sui generis*, are, in fact, liable to be extensively and profoundly influenced by psychoanalytical factors. Affectionate mothers, a stable psychological world, and gradual encouragement towards independence facilitate later confidence and success in learning; their absence impedes learning. Since children will vary widely in these respects, for their parents vary widely, one must expect that the more favoured children will adapt easily to new social and scholastic learning situations, while the least favoured, before they can progress further, may have to receive belated substitutes for what they have missed. The basic factors of affection, stability, and encouragement towards independence are the straw without which the bricks of later learning cannot be built.

The term 'psychoanalytical' has been used here with the loose connotation of 'being associated with some of the leading ideas of Freud and his followers'. One has to remember that Freud and his followers have sustained quite differing points of view; that much of the language of such writers (with its Ego, Id, and Superego, its 'transference' and 'introjection' and 'Oedipus Complex') is very much a *façon de parler*, a picturesque mythology quite different from clearly defined scientific terms; that there is no

decisive experimental evidence, but only clinical speculation, about certain parts of the theories (e.g. the nature
of infants' fantasies); that the psychoanalyst, like the
religious believer, expects one to swallow the faith whole
prior to understanding its justification; that it is very difficult to demonstrate scientifically the relationship between
infant experiences and later behaviour, although the evidence about the importance of maternal affection seems
plausibly established; that some psychologists of a more
behaviourist inclination would feel that their explanations
dealt adequately with psychoanalytical phenomena without resorting to the mythology of psychoanalytical
'explanations'; that sociologists and cultural anthropolo-
gists would criticize the neglect of *their* explanatory
concepts by *some* psychoanalysts; and that some non-
specialists have made psychoanalysis a facile plaything
which is far from the seriousness of its principal
exponents.

Despite this formidable list of reservations, there has
been something illuminating about psychoanalytic writings, even if it is not a scientific illumination. They have
turned attention to the power of mundane processes like
eating, excretion, and sex—forcing people to recognize
aspects of their psychological significance that were not
always recognized but also helping people to take more
moderate views of how these psychological factors can
be regulated, both in child-rearing and in adult life. Their
exploration of irrationality has been intended to free men,
in some degree, from irrationality by recognizing some of
its cruder and subtler forms and by indicating what kinds
of child-rearing are liable to impose fewer irrational impediments on new generations of children. Their emphasis
on the subconscious processes of the individual mind has
been developed and modified to take account of wider
biological, social, and cultural factors which determine
much of the interpretation or significance of the indi-

42

vidual's experience and behaviour. Their studies of some of the remoter or less obvious connections between superficially disparate items of experience or behaviour have encouraged the habit of keeping the whole man (and, of course, the whole learner) in view instead of looking at each item as if it were self-contained. And their demonstration, in detail, of how children's play and adults' social conversation provide a necessary means of working through personal emotional problems, in addition to any other purpose they may serve, has encouraged the wider use of these informal processes in education as well as in psychotherapy.

Sociological approaches

If the psychoanalyst invites one to search widely through the individual's psychological life to unearth vital connections that may not be immediately obvious, the sociologists invitation is to extend the field of reference particularly to the structure and influence of the social groups and institutions within which the individual grows up—the family and the roles which its members are expected to fulfil, the kinship grouping of which the family may be a part, the occupational and social class structures which partly shape the lives of the parents and their children in a great number of ways, the cultural values which prevail in the society or section of society to which the family belongs. How does the sociological compare with the psychoanalytical and behaviourist approaches? Where the psychoanalyst has sometimes seemed to envisage, even if not to substantiate, universal laws of psychological development, the sociologist, like the anthropologist, is apt to look at the cultural relativity suggested by the differing values of differing societies, or of different classes within one society. One society makes adolescence a period of tension and strife, another makes it a conventional transition from childhood to adult status.

43

One sanctions a prolonged tolerance of infant behaviour (breast-feeding, undisciplined excretory behaviour, etc.), another is impatient to get babies on to solid food and more convenient toilet habits.

Then, where the behaviourist has concerned himself with the experimental control of patterns of reinforcement shaping specific behaviour, the sociologist is concerned with the ways in which actual social institutions shape general ways of behaving. Behaviourist thinking (should one say 'behaviourist behaving'?) is anchored in physiology and in laboratory experiments, and directed, in practice, to detailed and specific learning programmes. Sociological thinking is anchored in its own sociological concepts (kinship, social stratification, value systems, etc.) and in statistical analysis of society, and directed, in practice, to appraisals of social policy. Both behaviourism and sociology provide, in a sense, theories of behaviour, but their conceptual frameworks are different and their practical implications are different. They may not be irreconcilable, but they represent different kinds of interest in people and different lines of attack on the understanding of them.

The Newsons' study of *Patterns of Infant Care in an Urban Community* (1965) is one example of a descriptive sociological approach to some of the problems of infant learning. It is based on home interviews with 709 Nottingham mothers of one-year-old children who answered questions about the upbringing of their children during the first year of life. The book is well worth studying in detail, both for its statistical analysis of data and for its entertaining accounts of the interviews. One of the most striking facts illustrated is the nature of the differences in child-rearing customs among the social classes studied. The difference can perhaps best be illustrated by Table I, which presents selected points of comparison between the top and bottom social classes (five class divisions in all having

44

been used). A study of the original would remind one that these are differences of emphasis. One has to note that most mothers, whatever their class, were not breast-feeding at six months; that a quarter of Class I mothers *were* using a dummy at twelve months; that 5 per cent of Class I babies were judged to be having a nutritionally inadequate diet; and so on.

TABLE I*

Child-rearing habits and social class

	Class I/II	Class V
	%	%
1. Mother 21 or less at first birth	24	53
2. Breast-feeding at 6 months	20	7
3. No bottle-feeding after 12 months	50	15
4. Dummy sometimes used at 12 months	26	46
5. Bedtime 8 pm or later	7	26
6. Sleeps in room alone	54	3
7. Diet inadequate	5	32
8. Potty training not started, 12 months	12	32
9. Genital play checked	25	93
10. High paternal participation in rearing	57	36

* This table is adapted, with acknowledgements to J. and E. Newson and George Allen and Unwin Ltd., from *Infant Care in An Urban Community*, p. 229.

One must remember too that these were the prevalent practices in one town at one time; they might differ in other times and places. And some of the differences might be associated with social conditions, whether good or bad, for which the mothers were not responsible but which were simply given. An interesting comparison is made between mothers who tend to be highly restrictive (24 per cent) and those tending to be permissive. Both would eventually pick up a crying baby to soothe it into silence. The restrictive mother would say to herself, 'he stopped crying as soon as I picked him up—so there was nothing wrong with him at all, he was just having me on.' The permissive mother would say, 'he stopped crying as soon as I picked him up—he must have needed me.' Of all the mothers, 62 per cent some-times smacked their baby, but the authors add the com-ment that 'the baby who is still unsmacked at a year has little reason to expect that this lenience will continue past the toddler age' (p. 205). The facts reported in the Newsons' study do not prove a great deal about learning, but they do remind one of a whole set of early training variables which presumably incline different children in different directions of development and at least colour their early conceptions of learning. Psychoanalytical theories would expect variations in things like severity of toilet-training to produce variations in later personal-ity, but this is not proven.

Sociologists and psychologists have given a new emphasis to the significance of language for infant and subsequent learning. Referring to a mid-1950s study of a Yorkshire coal-mining village, Klein (1965) mentions an anti-intellectualist trend and 'difficulty in handling any ideas which have not been absorbed into traditional vocabulary or phrasing'. Bernstein and others have ana-lysed some of the details of speech patterns in relation to learning. In educationally or socially handicapped families, sentences are short and simple, syntax is often poor and incomplete, conjunctions like *so*, *then*, or *be-cause* are used repetitively and often inaccurately, adjec-tives and adverbs are employed in a rigid and limited way, impersonal pronouns like *it* or *one* are infrequently used, and discourse tends to be categoric ('Do as I tell you!'). In families where speech matters are more sophisticated, there is more clarity and system, more reasons given for assertions or requests, more variety and precision in language, more generality and more impersonal assertions. These differences are obvious enough in themselves. What

46

is novel is the fuller realization that verbal differences are not just trivial and superficial variants of expression; they have been shown to be positive facilitators or impeders of substantial learning. Words alone are insufficient, but they are a means to substantial understanding of the world, and a means which culturally impoverished families do not supply. It seems necessary, therefore, to evolve, as suggested in an earlier section, culture-compensation programmes for culturally handicapped pre-school children.

One kind of sociocultural learning that is well begun in the pre-school years is what is called sex-typing. Mussen (1965, p. 286) mentions that two-year-old boys and girls hit, scream, and cry with about equal frequency, whereas, in one study, by four years of age, boys did more hitting and less screaming than the girls. Boys and girls learn to identify themselves with the objects, activities, and ideals that society teaches them to regard as appropriate to the respective sexes. Erikson (1965, p. 99) reports, with a psychoanalytic emphasis, on observed differences in the play behaviour of young boys and girls—'in the boys, the outstanding variables were height and downfall and strong motion (Indians, animals, motor cars) and its channelization or arrest (policemen); in girls, static interiors, which are open, simply enclosed, and peaceful or intruded upon. Boys adorned high structures; girls, gates.'

Perspective on pre-school learning

Specific aspects of pre-school learning must be seen against the general pattern of child development in these early years. No attempt is made here to present such a pattern as fully as is necessary. The student must go to one of the many published accounts of child development in infancy, including particularly the account given by Piaget, or, more easily, by one of his exponents, such as Flavell (1963) or Hunt (1961). Even the behaviourist, psychoanalytical, and sociological aspects of learning dealt with in this

47

chapter have only been introduced, not dealt with fully. This tends to confirm the earlier suggestion that learning is, indeed, a complex thing. One tries to spot simple beginnings in infancy, but, instead, discovers at once a series of widely ramifying influences, each of which, in its own way, shapes the child's learning—shapes it in infancy, and, thereby, begins to shape it in the subsequent period of schooling.

The infant's relationship with his mother (or mother-substitute) seems to be well established as a prime determiner of the child's development of self-assurance and confidence in the social world, with all the implications that these have for subsequent learning. The infant's opportunities to evolve a stable and satisfying sense of who and what he is, through other relationships in the family and through experience and mastery of the physical world, constitute a further step on the road to successful learning of every relevant kind. The cultural values of the family and the character of the language in which these values find their ordinary expression are also powerful determinants of the child's learning achievements, opening up wide horizons or narrowing life to a thin intellectual perspective. The child's learning is shaped by material and social rewards, operating perhaps on principles such as the behaviourists have described; but some psychologists also emphasize the manner in which the infant, from birth, builds up his own world, creates his own intellectual perspective, and is not just a resultant force of external pressures. Mothers who have experienced the 'will of his own' that even a baby seems to exert, may be very ready to believe this viewpoint. At five or six or seven, depending on the educational laws of the country concerned, the young child, already predisposed in a particular direction by all the factors described, confronts a new challenge—the transition from learning at home to learning at school.

48

3

Primary school learning

Some background considerations

Before looking more closely at the learning problems of
the young boy or girl in the new setting of the school,
it may be useful to make a kind of inventory of the considerations that it seems necessary to keep in mind
throughout the discussion. That is, it seems necessary to
keep them in the back of one's mind, even if only one or
two may have to be brought to the forefront for a particular part of the argument. The first chapter argued and
illustrated that any full study of learning should take
account of (i) the learners themselves, (ii) what they want
to or have to learn, (iii) the educational institutions and
the different contexts of learning they provide, (iv) any
specific teaching methods used, and (v) any specific learning methods used. The second chapter illustrated three
further different ways of looking at learning—(vi) the
behaviourist, (vii) the psychoanalytical, and (viii) the
sociological. These represent different emphases, different
angles of vision, not completely distinct or mutually exclusive categories.

Several more items should be added to the inventory—
again, items that are partly distinct but that also partly
overlap with others. Although the concern here is with
learning, one can never afford to forget (ix) the general

patterns of physical, emotional, social, and intellectual development that can be detected by observing children over periods of time. Although these patterns are obviously shaped by learning, there are at least relative limits to what patterns can emerge at any age. There are minimal ages before which virtually no one expects babies to walk, or talk, or control their bladders, or show any sustained interest in other infants. Similarly, there are minimal ages before which one does not expect most children to be able to read or count, to play co-operatively with other children, to sustain interest in a scholastic task for a long time, to have any sense of time let alone of other historical abstractions, or to subscribe to moral standards except in the sense of being enticed or compelled to behave as adults decide they should. Between the ages of about five and twelve children move gradually from a developmental stage in which the action or image of the moment dominates thinking, and where personal fancy and objective reality are not clearly distinguished, to a developmental stage in which most begin to see things at least with a degree of objectivity. But at every stage the range of variation among individuals is wide.

Another background consideration is (x) the different perspectives on primary (or other) school learning that one must expect to find in teachers, parents, administrators, and politicians. Because teachers are the largest group likely to study deliberately, out of professional concern, the processes of learning, there is some tendency to look at learning too narrowly in terms of class-room teaching. The teacher tends to be preoccupied with how she will manage to teach in the specific circumstances given to her; the parent with how to get for his child the best available schooling; the administrator with evolving workable dispositions of staff, buildings, and other resources within the remit given him by the law and his employers; the politician largely with the defence and propagation of his party's policy, and, whatever his party, with national aspects of social, political, and economic policy and their bearing on the educational system as a whole. One could exemplify other special perspectives on learning (for example, the headmaster's, psychologist's, or sociologist's), but what is being emphasized is that problems appearing to the teacher as problems of school learning may arise really outside the school, be understandable only in a context wider than that of classroom or school, and be soluble only by measures taken outside the classroom or school.

This last point reminds one naturally of (xi) the need— especially for teachers whose own learning may have been relatively academic in its emphasis—to think of learning in terms of skills and attitudes, and not only in terms of knowledge, despite the importance of the latter. Furthermore, it is useful to remember the extent to which skills, attitudes, and knowledge are acquired outside of any school programme. School learning and learning outside school are both very important. Skills, attitudes, and knowledge are all important. All of these are complexly interrelated. It is pointless to magnify one or detract from another. No one of these planks alone makes an educational platform. Although these remarks may appear to be truistic, student-teachers sometimes repudiate what they like to call 'mere factual knowledge' as an educational diet for students but are surprised to find that primary school children too have a limited appetite for the factual diet offered them by the less experienced student-teacher. Perhaps at both levels the problem is one of respecting factual knowledge but at the same time connecting it more dynamically with the development of skills and attitudes. Students who have not themselves experienced this kind of connection are, obviously, more likely to think of all learning as being 'scholastic' in an unfortunately narrow sense of that word.

The last consideration that is recommended for this

back-of-the-mind inventory is (xii) the great variety of the evidence that is relevant to understanding primary school learning. Much of the evidence derives from the accumulated experience and criticism of those practically concerned with school learning. Such evidence has to be sifted to determine where it points to some useful degree of generality and where its relevance is only local or temporary; where it is cogently argued and, therefore, useful at least within its own context, and where it is logically or informationally defective even within its own limits; where it has all the signs of being just a bee in some person's (or some group's communal) bonnet and where it appears to be a relatively unprejudiced attempt to assess or deal with an educational situation. This may sound rather like finding one's way through quicksands, but one cannot usefully analyse educational problems without having some serious regard to the general character of the ongoing educational enterprise. To do so is not enough, but it is necessary—if only (at its lowest) to enable one to 'sell' policies derived from harder evidence, that is, from evidence that is exact, comprehensive, and reliable.

The harder evidence is not as hard or as copious as that of the physical sciences, but it at least refines 'common sense'. For many aspects of development and learning it is possible to define, via tests and observations, the average performance and the range of performance that can be expected for a particular age group in a particular cultural environment in a particular period of time. The degree of association between these various performances and circumstances can often be stated quantitatively, even if that association still needs to be explained in a more fundamental way. Various forms of statistically controlled experiment and of statistical analysis of data make it possible to sift out explanations so that some are seen to be more valid than others, even if the surviving explanations are not the last word on the subject. An example from the Plowden Report on *Children and Their Primary Schools* (1967, vol. 2, p. 181) is the evidence leading to the conclusion that 'the variation in parental attitudes can account for more of the variation in children's school achievement than either the variation in home circumstances or the variation in schools', and that 'among the school variables of which we took notice the most important appeared to be the quality of the teaching'.

Although statistical survey and analysis is a characteristic feature of evidence about learning, it is expensive and technically inconvenient even to sample all of the evidence that might be relevant at any time. The choice of sampling is bound to be influenced by prior value judgements about what *seems* worth studying. One must, therefore, look at even the hard evidence about learning for concealed or disguised assumptions about values and for extrapolations of apparent trends beyond the evidence actually available. Variations in value systems from culture to culture and from generation to generation militate against universal laws of learning. However, just as it has been said that 'all are equal but some more so than others', perhaps too some generalizations about learning are 'more universal than others'.

The learners and what they have to learn

It might be useful to pass a law banning those interested in education from using the expression 'the child'. They would always have to say 'children' and specify which categories of children they were speaking about—the ten-year-old daughters of London stockbrokers, the six-year-old sons of New York negroes, the Scottish children of eleven who got an above-average score on X's intelligence test, a random sample of eight-year-old English children in 1965, and so on. If they really meant 'the child' they would have to name him or her—Jerry Bloggs or Mary

Sproggs. Since customary usage dies hard, one had better simply reiterate that children vary immensely and that a great deal of the variation in learning can be accounted for in terms of certain constantly recurring factors, for example, age, sex, intelligence (however defined or constituted), temperamental stability and disposition, national and local culture (in the sociological or anthropological sense), the historical period at which the culture is considered, the socio-economic status of the particular family or social group, the prevailing attitudes of the parents to their children and to school learning, and the quality of school teaching available. Moreover, it is important to consider the operation of these factors not just at one point in time for a given set of children, but over a longer period of time. Some variation, such as the tendency of young girls to be linguistically more advanced than boys, may be quite important for the period when it operates but fade into lesser significance over a longer stretch of time. One has to deal with both perspectives—the immediate or short-term and the long-term.

As long ago as 1931 the Hadow report on The Primary School provided a broad characterization of primary school children which is still apposite. It speaks of:

> the necessity of correcting the effects of earlier weaknesses, and of building up reserves of health to meet the stress of adolescence; the wide variations in intelligence shown even by the age of five, and the consequent need for careful classification; the necessity of avoiding over-intellectualization and of keeping within narrow limits any kind of instruction which imposes a severe strain on the attention; the large place which should be given to games, singing, dancing, drawing, acting and craftmanship; the importance of cultivating the imagination, of appealing to the emotions, and of fostering the social spirit.

It continues:

> Any education worthy of the name must start from the facts, and the essential facts are, after all, simple. At the age when they attend the primary schools, children are active and inquisitive, delighting in movement, in small tasks that they can perform with deftness and skill, and in the sense of visible and tangible accomplishment which such tasks offer; intensely interested in the character and purpose—the shape, form, colour and use —of the material objects around them; at once absorbed in creating their own miniature world of imagination and emotion, and keen observers who take pleasure in reproducing their observations by speech and dramatic action; and still engaged in mastering a difficult and unfamiliar language, without knowing that they are doing so, because it is a means of communicating with other human beings. These activities are not aimless, but form the process by which children grow. They are, in a very real sense, their education; and the course of wisdom for the educationalist is to build upon them (*The Primary School*, 1931, pp. xvi, xvii).

How does the characterization and prescription of Hadow in 1931 compare with those of Plowden in 1967 —thirty-six years later? Plowden emphasizes the wide variability of children in physical and intellectual development, the fact that more girls now reach puberty in the last years of primary school (Douglas, 1966, p. 78, instances 17 per cent of a sample of eleven-year-old girls), the extensive interaction of hereditary and environmental effects, and the differences among socio-economic classes (for example, of one inch in average height between five-year-olds from upper middle class and unskilled workers' homes respectively). The report mentions (i) the possible transfer of parent-child relationships, along psychoanalytical lines, to teacher-child relationships, (ii) children's strong autonomous drive 'towards activity and exploration of the environment' together with curiosity about novel and un-expected features of his (any child's) experience', (iii) 'the pressure in the young child towards the emergence of sensori-motor skills', (iv) 'individual differences between children in level of ability, sensitivity, vigour and tempo of response', (v) the central role of spoken language in learning and (vi) the influence on personality of 'different ways of upbringing and cultural expectations' and of 'expectations and practices derived from the family relationship'.

Chapters 16 and 17 on Children Learning in School and Aspects of the Curriculum stress the interconnection of work and play, the idea that 'the child is the agent in his own learning' (p. 194), and the importance of providing materials and opportunities of learning rather than a forced or stereotyped programme. Primary school French and science are relatively new features on the menu, repre-senting a further broadening of the curriculum since Hadow's days. A steady advance in standards of primary school reading between 1948 and 1964 is recorded, as is a persisting difference of opinion between those who would and would not maintain the customary pattern of religious education in primary schools. Perhaps the biggest differ-ence in the modern report is its major concern with the so-called 'educational priority areas', and, more generally, with the principle of 'compensatory education'—the idea that, by positive governmental policy, certain areas which are socially and educationally handicapped (or disadvant-aged, to use the vogue word), may be given specially favourable treatment to make up for their disadvantage. This particularly highlights the new tendency to look at learning problems, not only in pedagogic terms (although Hadow and Plowden largely see eye to eye in this area) but in terms of education by social policy and contrived structural management. One does not just attempt to train better drivers : one gives them, or persuades them to build, new or modified vehicles, so that the educational journey cannot (at least, in theory) but be more profitable.

The conception of primary school children that emerges from reports like Plowden is a rather hybrid one—a bit of tradition, a bit of common sense, a bit of general psychology, a bit of social policy, all mixed up together. This may be intrinsic to the situation, for one can only study children as they are influenced by the varying cultural patterns that prevail at different times, and any national policy-making or policy-guiding body can hardly escape from its own most fundamental national assumptions. This is illustrated in the Plowden report's remarkable comment on the occasional eagerness of immigrant children for formal learning : 'this eagerness sometimes proves an embarrassment when it is for the disciplined book-learning and formal instruction of their own culture and when the language barrier prevents the school explaining fully to parents the different way we go about education in England' ! Different kinds of learning opportunity are distributed to different categories of children according to customary national and local patterns, or according to newly applied policies which modify traditional ways. These opportunities, which are bound to vary even in the most egalitarian community, partly determine what and how children learn.

Although there is an arbitrary element in many of the possible ways of categorizing primary school children, there is always one category, however defined, which needs special consideration—that of 'slow learners'. It is quite difficult to keep up with the varying names given to the category, for educators keep inventing new names for it, as each successive name becomes tarnished with the problems and failures of the children concerned. The laudable desire to avoid any name suggesting defect or failure tends to conflict with a clear recognition that 'slow learning' is a substantial educational and social handicap in our kind of society and that the more extreme forms of it are singularly demanding on the time and patience of teachers, particularly when material educational resources are poorly supplied. The Plowden report uses the term 'slow learners' of 'children who are genetically poorly endowed as well as those of average ability who are seriously retarded in their attainments' (p. 301) and mentions that the Department of Education and Science has estimated that 'approximately one child in every ten aged over seven is sufficiently retarded to need special education, though this number is significantly greater in some areas'.

There is, of course, no sharp division between slow learners as just defined and the 10 or 15 per cent just above them, who are still slow learners compared with the middle range of children. Indeed, as one moves towards the average there may be an increasing tendency to expect at least an average learning performance, even with a below-average learning capacity. Within limits, such an expectation need not be wholly bad, for expectations influence performance, provided they are not hopelessly beyond reach; but the learning programme should be restrained in scope and speed to give an encouraging opportunity to those in the lowest quarter or third of the learning range. This means, particularly, that there should be no rigidity in the expectations of different stages—for example, an expectation that the transition from infant to junior class at seven, or from primary to secondary school at eleven or twelve, will miraculously make slow learners capable of coping with new standards and methods. At each transition teachers must accept double responsibility—to provide a fresh challenge to the ablest by all means, but also to sustain the thread of encouragement which, at a humbler level, will prevent the slow learner from giving up the educational enterprise alto-

58

gether and accepting the defeated role and derogatory stigmata which teachers (and society acting through them) foist upon him.

As children move through the primary school they move from a stage at which much allowance is made for their limitations and individual requirements to a stage at which teachers, parents, and society generally, expect them to have mastered the elementary aspects of the reading, writing, and counting skills, to have some beginnings of general knowledge and understanding of the world in which they live, and to have developed attitudes which will help them to get on with other people and with their own further education. Although, at eleven or twelve, they are still children, they are normally much more independent children compared with the five-year-olds entering school, of whom one quarter might show signs of distress at the very fact of leaving their mothers, and of whom 5 per cent might continue to feel distressed for a month or more (Plowden, vol. 2, p. 245). The primary school offers children fresh horizons, whether those traditionally opened up by mastery of the three Rs or any others, varying with the prevalent or fashionable theories of primary school curriculum. But the school is obviously not the sole medium of learning. In the family, in the neighbourhood, in travel and play, knowledge, skills, and attitudes are learned which confirm, or conflict with, those acquired in school.

Institutions of primary school learning

Blyth (1965) has given one of the most comprehensive and well-balanced sociological accounts of English primary schools. He analyses them in terms of (1) *social structure* (formal, semi-formal, and informal), (2) *social function* (instruction, socialization, classification, welfare, and autonomy), (3) *social cohesion and control* (norms, rules, and positive maintenance of social control), and (4) *social change*. This kind of analysis is related to three educational traditions—(a) the *elementary*, deriving from the kind of state school perpetuated by the 1870 Education Act, narrowly utilitarian in its atmosphere; (b) the *preparatory*, associated with social exclusiveness and orientation towards entry into the independent, fee-paying boarding schools at about the age of thirteen; and (c) the *developmental*, associated with the idea of educating children in accordance with what are taken to be their own developmental 'needs' (a question-begging word, of course) rather than with any stereotyped pattern imposed by tradition or society.

The three educational traditions mentioned cannot be discussed fully here, but such traditions, whatever their nature, must form an essential part of the study of anyone who wants to understand the school system in any country. Such traditions reflect important aspects of the society itself and are powerfully perpetuated via actual buildings, curricula, family and class custom, relationships between the schools and other educational institutions, patterns of teacher-training (or non-training), segregated professional organizations for different groups of teachers, and all the other institutionalized phenomena which define a tradition in substantial terms. The content and context of learning obviously vary more or less as one or other tradition prevails, although several traditions may vie with one another in what is nominally one kind of school. For example, a public primary school may embody the developmental tradition in its infant classes, the elementary tradition among any of its teachers who still see themselves as mainly purveyors of the four Rs, and the preparatory tradition among those who excel as crammers for the academic stream of the secondary school.

A feature of the social structure and function of many English primary schools that has caused considerable controversy is the division (or 'streaming') of pupils of the same year-group into separate classes according to apparent academic ability when there are more children than one class can cater for. This practice, although intended to minister to scholastic efficiency, is felt by some to represent a socially divisive policy, for middle-class children are more likely to be recruited into the A stream and the children of lower social classes into the B or C streams. Moreover, streaming is also alleged to be unfair educationally, for those who already have educational advantages through their home upbringing receive more through their schooling, while those with existing disadvantages have an inferior educational image foisted upon them at school. The evidence about the influence of streaming on attainments and attitudes is not conclusive but many would agree with Blyth that 'for most schools where numbers require subdivision, random or "equated" allocation may bring the best balance of advantage' (p. 65). Blyth is more careful than some to mention various factors, such as the problems of slow learners or of teachers less skilled in group work, which remind one that non-streaming does not miraculously solve all the practical problems of good primary education.

Blyth makes considerable use of the evidence of sociometry—the technique of investigating social preferences by asking children to name who they would most like to sit beside, whose team they would prefer not to be in, and other questions of this kind. He also draws on more general observational evidence about the various roles that children enter, or are thrust into, during their primary schooling. There seems to be a certain stability in such roles. Once the class decides that Mary is good at art or Tommy good at being a buffoon, that Ernest is a terrific centre-forward or Elizabeth a little actress, then these roles tend to be upheld so far as possible, although they may originate in chance events. Athletic or other non-scholastic

61

prowess earns its own esteem in the 'alternative value' system that parallels the world of scholastic success and failure. Children also inject their own norms into the school system, especially where a group live together in the same area and are, therefore, able to sustain their own values more readily in their leisure hours.

'Autonomy' as a social function of the school refers to the possibility that an individual school, within the general pattern of school functions, may establish its own distinctive personality—whether it is associated with liveliness in music or art, or particular friendliness towards parents, or any other such feature. Blyth goes so far as to say that:

> if there is one idea embedded in this book which is essentially prescriptive rather than descriptive in character . . . it is that a primary school realizes itself and its roles most fully through the building of an autonomous culture based on the arts, within which role-playing can be developed without the restrictions of social class, the veto of social custom or the barrier of stereotype (p. 192).

This is a quite ambitious ideal, depending considerably on the headmaster, but also on the teachers with their varied roles as instructor, parent-substitute, organizer, value-bearer, classifier, and welfare worker—a 'role-complex' which puts a strain on some teachers to decide what they are mainly supposed to be.

A primary school can obviously be influenced by social change in various ways—by movements of population from city slum to suburban housing estate, by pressures towards egalitarianism as exemplified by public policies of 'comprehensive' secondary education, or by national movements for curricular reform which bring French, science, or 'new mathematics' on to the primary school scene. Is the primary school itself simply a vehicle of social change?

Or can it, in any sense, be considered an instigator of such change? Perhaps that is not the way to put it. It obviously is a vehicle of social change instigated elsewhere, but it perhaps does the schools less than justice to use the phrase *simply a vehicle*. To be a vehicle of such things as the 'developmental' outlook or the new curricular outlook requires instigatory activity at least at the local level. Then, if one has regard to Blyth's autonomous function of the primary school, it might be held that this often means instigating social change, again, at least within the local context.

To develop any subtlety in appraising the institutional side of primary school learning it is obviously desirable to look at different national cultures and different sub-cultures within nations, and to study these historically as well as in contemporary terms. Although we can speak glibly of primary schools, the conception of dividing school education into primary and secondary is not very old. The 1870 elementary school that catered for the whole education of most children was still represented by a few surviving 'all-age' schools until quite recently. Most German children still get most of their education in a *Volkschule* that provides a general education from six to fifteen. Even as England has been getting accustomed to primary education referring to the ages five to eleven, some educationists have begun to propose other divisions, including a conceivable middle school from nine to thirteen. Although primary school French, mathematics, science, and sex, have arrived, their rationale is often understood only in general terms and one could imagine some new emphases in a few decades. But, however shifting the ground, the institutions of learning deserve study as much as the learners for whom they cater.

Methods of teaching and learning in primary schools

D. E. M. Gardner's *Experiment and Tradition in Primary Schools* (1966) provides a good introduction to the problems and achievements of those who have attempted to make an experimental comparison of two of the main approaches to primary school children and their learning. The comparison is made by observing and testing children in several pairs of schools over a period of years. In each pair of schools, one was characterized by the fact that it was 'organized entirely on a subject basis' and that 'no definite attempt was made in such schools to break away from established tradition', while the other school of each matched pair 'made some definite departure from a wholly subject-orientated time-table' (Gardner, p. 30). Apart from this difference in attitude or emphasis, both schools of each pair were well taught within their own contexts. The children were matched by age, intelligence, sex, and social background, so that, as far as possible, these factors would not contribute to any learning differences between the two groups. At the age of six or seven, and again at ten, tests of attainments and of attitudes were given to the paired groups, to see how the 'experimental' classes compared with their traditional 'controls'.

The ten-year-old 'experimentals' were 'undoubtedly superior' in tests of (a) listening and remembering, (b) neatness, care, and skill, (c) ingenuity, (d) free drawing and painting, (e) English, including original composition and (f) interests; and they were rather better too in tests of (g) social situation, (h) concentration on an uninteresting task, (i) moral judgement, (j) general information, (k) reading, and (l) handwriting. The 'experimentals' were not significantly different from the 'controls' in (m) concentration on a self-chosen task, (n) results on a social distance scale, and (o) moral conduct, and were not quite so good in (p) mechanical arithmetic, or (q) problem arithmetic. Proponents of child-centred rather than subject-centred education would claim that such results show that there is little, if any, scholastic loss and considerable attitudinal gain in a programme of child-centred learning.

It is obviously difficult to establish control of all the variables in a study like that just described. There are problems of deciding whether a school is 'experimental' in the required sense. Schools keep changing in one way or another even over short periods of time. Subtle factors, such as the way parental attitude influences children's learning even within the same socio-economic class, are difficult to reckon with. There are obvious problems about making reliable assessments of things like attitudes or moral conduct. There is a problem of assessing the indirect influence of the prevalent beliefs of the researchers, whether it is a Gardner researching into primary schooling with a faith in a certain kind of child-centred education or a Bereiter researching into compensatory nursery education and advocating 'selecting specific and significant educational objectives and teaching them in the most direct manner possible, as is done in the intermediate and secondary school grades' (Hechinger, p. 106). Despite these reservations, Gardner's researches, conducted with great persistence and care in the face of difficulties, at least tend to moderate the animus of anyone who might be tempted, in the language of the headlines, to 'rap' child-centred education.

The actual term 'child-centred' has been a useful slogan to sum up a particular corrective emphasis in education— a revolt against practices such as the lecture-question-and-answer lesson, the fixed time-table and narrow curriculum, and teacher dominance of the class situation by voice and disciplinary sanction; a move towards increasing the amount and variety of activities and experience that children get, to more extended projects centred on matters that interest the children and involving the use of several skills towards one general purpose over a given time, to encouraging self-direction within the current project, and to creating learning rather than directly instructional situations. Child-centredness is still a good slogan for one necessary part of the educational enterprise, but it stands more firmly if not mistaken for a complete theory of education.

A complete educational policy has to be teacher-centred and culture-centred as well as child-centred, if one may impose so many centres on the geometry of the educational situation. By 'teacher-centred' is meant that teachers should have, not a diminished role but an equally strong and different role—that of learning-planner rather than instruction-giver, although still properly an instructor to some extent. By 'culture-centred' is meant that the knowledge, skills, and attitudes of a society are not entirely casual acquisitions. They come down to each new generation, hard-won by their predecessors, subtly ordered and expressed in the media of language and literature, mathematics and science, religion, music, and all the other major modes of human creation and experience. A teacher who was, *per impossibile*, completely child-centred would be a moronic person to put in charge of children. She, like her young charges, must, according to their respective levels, learn what is worth while learning, however subtly the beginner may be led on to the cultural scene. Although the complex interrelation of child, teacher, and culture in the learning situation seems very obvious, this has not prevented some from writing as if one leg, or two, of the tripos would hold the learner up.

One could understand someone wanting to banish the word 'methods' from discussions of teaching and learning. It has so often carried a connotation of authoritarian prescription and sometimes of obsession with a single prescription, regardless of differences among children, teachers, schools, and cultural evaluations of what is worth learning. Even allowing for variety of methods, it

66

may suggest that there *is* a variety of methods which have been substantially validated by experiment or deduction from well-established theory, whereas any such validation is often, in practice, imperfect or well watered down with considerations of expediency, tradition, or social policy. If one turns to psychology for theoretical support one finds that at least some of the learning theorists (in the psychologist's sense) disclaim any suggestion of being able to offer theoretically well-founded advice about specific human learning problems. If one considers the extent to which learning is determined by various socio-economic and familiar factors, it may seem that 'method' in any narrower sense is a feeble runner alongside these giants. How, then, can one lay a foundation for the idea or 'method' in teaching or learning?

Three approaches seem useful. The most precise and restricted would be concerned with comparing experimentally the results of two or more specific techniques of achieving a specific scholastic result and determining which was most effective. The most general, although not necessarily imprecise, would be concerned with the broadest possible view of 'method', so that it included all the evidence and factors one would take into account in implementing an educational policy—whether for a person, a class, a school, or a society. Psychology, economics, politics, and many other factors might be brought into the reckoning, depending on the nature of the educational problem posed. The third view of method lies between the first two. It would accept the wider context as it stood (as most teachers must) and explore for plausible connections between particular learning problems and any general psychological or sociological theories that threw light on them—even if it were only the light of analogy, which suggests but does not prove. If method does not mean (1) experimentally proven technique, or (2) a comprehensively and consistently planned means of effectively implementing some agreed policy, or (3) teaching and learning practices buttressed by relevant principles of general psychology or sociology, then it would appear to mean, residually, (4) individual inclination in matters of educational implementation—personal style almost.

Techniques which have been studied experimentally include 'streaming', non-subject-orientated time-tabling, intensive arithmetical and other coaching at the ages of ten and eleven, early and late starts to instruction in reading, the initial teaching alphabet as an aid to first steps in reading, different methods of teaching children to subtract, and programmed learning. Such studies, which cannot be briefly summarized in the present context, have provided useful guidance in many aspects of classroom method. The more specific they are, the less can one expect universal rules to emerge from them, but they have disproved some assumptions and demonstrated the relevance of others at least to particular groups of learners. They have suggested economies in some learning processes and ways of avoiding learner-frustration. Method in the second sense—of implementing policy—has been sufficiently stressed already where attention has been drawn to the many extra-scholastic factors that shape learning. Headmasters and other administrators obviously have a special responsibility for establishing the atmosphere, relationships, and material facilities which can support children's learning or, if absent, undermine it. This is an area of great power, with corresponding possibilities of triumph or frustration. Because class teachers wield such a limited amount of power in this area, especially where Heads sustain an autocratic tradition (however benevolent), there is a tendency to turn away from it and expect from classroom techniques alone more than they can possibly achieve in ordinary circumstances.

The third sense of method is one of the potentially most helpful to the classroom teacher—suggesting fruitful approaches to some learning problems and making others tolerable through understanding, even if not entirely soluble through lack of the necessary supporting structures. One of the main general principles in this category is that one must reinforce any pattern of behaviour which it is desired to strengthen and establish firmly. Learning must in general, even if not in every particular, be a rewarding experience, for children and adults alike simply do not bother to learn what does not reward them in any sense. Blyth (1965) argues that primary school children are very ready, on the whole, to identify themselves with the school society and to fulfil 'the good pupil role' if only they can. But, sometimes, by harsh transitional experiences from infant to junior school, by scholastic demands inadequately related to individual capacities, and by images of failure stamped upon those who may indeed be failing by some standards—by such means, learning is punished in some, and, most likely, those who have least encouragement to learning from their extra-scholastic environment. At least a considerable number of teachers require opportunities of learning themselves how to engineer some modest degree of success for slow learners, so that they do not, in their frustration as teachers, sustain frustration in the slow learners.

Alongside the principle of exploiting all means of positively rewarding learning, one might put the principle of recognizing the dynamic, transforming character of human mentality. Centuries of teachers have operated to a quite different conception—that, by drill and rote-learning, combined with punishment for failure to reproduce the drilled formula, one could force learning into children. A form of this pedagogy is still quite common in academic secondary schools with their dictated notes to get pupils through school-leaving examinations, even if the cane is replaced by non-acceptance into college as the punishment for poor memorizing. Examiners, if they look for textbook examination answers, obviously subscribe to the same xerographic conception of the human mind. Many psychologists have studied and demonstrated most clearly how the mind (or brain, if one prefers to be physiological) is a constant transformer, converting sensory inputs in accordance with its own operations. Obviously, we should communicate with one another even worse than we already do if there was not a considerable possibility of achieving common inputs, transformations, and outputs. This is part of what the discipline of study consists in. But variability is intrinsic to these operations, producing flashes of genius on the one hand and lapses into sheer error on the other.

Among primary school children the variability just mentioned operates at a yet more limiting level, for it is only in the senior years of the primary school that children are beginning to free themselves from the dominance of perceptual impressions ('which is heavier—a pound of wool or a pound of lead?') and to be able to handle reversible operations ($8+7=15$ the same as $15-7=8$). Operating with more abstract concepts, without concrete reference, comes later still. Adult conceptions of geography, history, or morality, themselves often imperfect and inconsistent enough, are still further beyond the reach of primary school children. The children will be more at home with what is sensible and particular, with possibilities of imitation and action, and transformation according to the patterns of the child's mind (or cortex). They will understand better what they see, hear, and handle while simultaneously and gradually being given the linguistic and other skills which sharpen and guide that understanding.

A third major learning principle, along with behavioural reinforcement and the idea of dynamic transformation, is that of devising the right structure for learning to take place. It is fairly clear that learning effects do not automatically transfer themselves beyond their original context. If one wants learning to generalize, it must be helped on its way by making the cross-references explicit and practising the learners in such cross-references. Many school systems are almost guarantees of non-transferred learning because of rigid teacher or subject divisions without provision for deliberate mutual reference. Even within one subject it is necessary to practise the various important combinations of elements if the learners are to develop fluency in relating the elements according to the requirements of different problems or situations. Principles of transfer or generalization must be made explicit. Transfer must be practised in order to become customary. In the primary school, the fact that a child deals with fewer teachers at a time, and that projects exercise several skills simultaneously (where project methods prevail), together help to encourage the generalizing of learning, but many schools have also had traditions of compartmentalized subjects and 'teaching for transfer' has meant teaching for 'transfer' examinations rather than transfer of learning in the sense of this paragraph.

For centuries men have been tantalized by the possibility of structuring learning situations so that learning should take place almost automatically, almost despite any inclination for it. This is exemplified in the long tradition of encyclopaedism, attempting to contain and systematize all knowledge, or at least much knowledge, within a few volumes; in the seventeenth-century pansophic ideal of purveying all knowledge to all men by the systematic teaching techniques propagated by Comenius; in modern programmed learning, with its precise definition of what is to be learned and its step-by-step stimulation of the learner to make the necessary responses. Examples of structural aspects of learning in primary schools might include, among others, various kinds of text-books, sets of mathematical apparatus (Dienes, Cuisenaire, etc.), class reference libraries, school time-tables (traditionally directed to sustaining particular emphases among different aspects of school work), maps and models, rules of classroom procedure, and even particular patterns of professional training of primary school teachers. Leith quotes examples of the successful use of programmed learning with children of primary school age (Leith, 1966, pp. 85-6).

It is a matter of common sense that structure is a key aspect of educational method. Common sense is underlined by the demonstrations by Piaget and his followers of how children do tend to structure their experience at different ages and how certain structures—for example, those associated with abstract analysis of hypothetical ideas—are irrelevant to the earlier ages represented by the primary school. Other psychological studies have illustrated how learning can be improved by such structural devices as spacing out different occasions of learning, by putting different rather than similar learning material into adjacent periods of learning, by extra practice of material that is to stay learnt for a longer period of time, and by practising the required responses in appropriate situations (for example, active recall of material without referring to books or notes) rather than unrequired responses in an irrelevant situation (for example, simply repeatedly reading through notes, if one will ultimately be required to write examination answers without notes; or practising examination answers, if one will ultimately be tested in a different kind of performance).

Lindgren's short discussion of Phenomenological Concepts of Learning (*Educational Psychology in the Classroom*, 1962, pp. 246-52) might be a starting point for correcting an excessive faith in structure as outlined so far. One has to remember (a great sorrow for all teachers) that neat and cogent structuring in the teacher's mind does not necessarily mean a corresponding achievement by the learner. One need not abandon the idea of structure, but one must include in it the structure of the pupil's interests, experience, and mentality generally. No amount of clarity will make a philosopher out of a primary school child, or, indeed, make him into anything that cannot be geared to his actual personality and experience. At the same time, given the stated condition of personal significance and involvement, a greater economy of learning can be achieved by clarity, repetition, multiple illustration, cross-reference, and other structural devices. And, if teachers are to give children the amount of individual consideration that idealists rightly, if optimistically, prescribe, they must concern themselves with the economy of class learning, not just of some non-existent Rousseauistic situation with one child and his personal tutor. This is obviously a large subject in its own right but one could begin by considering some of the ideas about time-wasting in the Scottish 1946 Report on Primary Education (paragraphs 104-8), including the reference to '(1) devices for keeping a class quiet and busy, (2) "correction" in its many forms, and (3) continued use of books that have lost their appeal and much of their usefulness'.

Perspective on primary school learning

Children between the ages of five or six and eleven or twelve probably have not excited the intense psychological interest that has been concentrated on the preceding period of infancy or the succeeding period of adolescence. Perhaps the primary school period is not as bad as the historical Dark Ages used to be—almost a millennium mercifully (for schoolboys) dropped into oblivion between the Roman Empire and the Renaissance—but it is still less susceptible of dramatic summing up than the other two periods. In relation to infancy, it is a period of social expansion—beyond the confines of the family into the peer group of the local community and into the sphere of influence of teachers, representing the state's best inten-

tions for the socialization of its young members. In rela
tion to adolescence, it is a period of fundamental and
necessary preparation—a preparation that is partly just
growing up in encouraging circumstances (at least, they
should be encouraging) and partly acquiring the particular
attitudes, skills, and knowledge on which secondary education must be based.

Because primary schooling is based on strongly articu-
lated conceptions of deliberate education it throws up a
host of very particular problems. How should children be
grouped in school? How should reading and arithmetic
be taught? How should slow learners be catered for? What
subjects should have a place in the curriculum and with
what relative emphasis on each? What general teaching
methods and attitudes should be fostered? How should
parents and teachers be brought into most fruitful co-
operation (if this is accepted as desirable)? What examinations or tests should be employed, and when? How can
gross social inequalities among different school districts
be modified so that all children receive a sufficiently good
education? How should primary school teachers and headmasters or headmistresses be prepared for their work?
These are some of the obvious questions, and others can
be pursued through the pages of the various modern
reports and books on primary education. Any one such
question needs to be discussed in great detail if one is
working out practical policies. The present perspective
must be broader, emphasizing only general (but still quite
definite) principles.

It is tempting to begin with one more reaffirmation of
the fact that children vary enormously and that the variations are determined by the many complex factors mentioned in earlier parts of this chapter. The practical significance of this is that one must expect statements about
primary learning to be surrounded with ifs and buts. At
the same time there are many generalizations that are

quite well established and have a fair degree of generality in their application. Several of these have been discussed. Where applied, they have made primary education different from what it often was and, one could readily argue, better. Many aspects of primary education, however, represent particular evaluations of what is worth while for children between five and twelve in a particular society. An analysis of primary school learning must therefore look to varieties of tradition and value as well as to varieties of psychological or educational method.

Recognizing the need for a complex rather than any too simple model of primary school learning, one might then think in terms of matching several different kinds of structure—(1) the children's varying maturational structure (all that the many studies of childhood have clarified), (2) the varying structure of the local and national society (all that sociological analyses have clarified), (3) the structure of the knowledge, skills and attitudes that primary schools are concerned to develop (once mainly the four Rs, now a more varied diet), and (4) the structure of the machinery of schooling itself (particular kinds of building, equipment, teacher-training, school administration, learning method, etc.). Obviously there are many defensible ways of matching such complex things. The principle suggested is that any philosophy of primary education, however rudimentary, should take account of each of the main areas just listed. Given a particular school (or set of schools) in a particular society with a particular set of social and educational traditions, what learning should one aim to achieve and how can one best achieve it? What aims or methods are desirable and practicable for the immediate future? What longer-term changes in any of the structures (buildings, books, methods, administration, etc.) are desirable and practicable? What are the criteria or touchstones of desirability? What are the criteria of practicability in relation to any proposed policy?

75

Allowing a complex model and the approach to policy-making just outlined, what further principle might hold out hope of individual efficiency or significance to any one practically involved in helping primary school children to learn? Perhaps the answer has something to do with the last of four senses of educational method mentioned earlier—that of individual or personal style. Not to study the structural factors just discussed is obscurantist, but structure is tidier on paper than in practical operation. Just as each school may have an autonomous factor of the kind described by Blyth, so each teacher in a school, however hemmed in by material, administrative, or traditional restrictions, has at least a small measure of potential autonomy. It may even be not so small, for what is vaguely called the teacher's 'personality' is longest remembered when everything else may be 'forgotten'—not really forgotten entirely, but absorbed so as to be indistinguishable. It might be an interesting question to consider how much primary school learning owes to this factor of personal style down the ages to our own day and how much to psychological, sociological, and educational analysis.

4

Secondary school learning

The significance of secondary schooling

The idea of secondary schooling is, of course, very man-made and arbitrary. It implies a developed system of education structured into several stages. But the stages may be quite different in different times and places. The old German *Gymnasium* took selected pupils through an academic curriculum between the ages of 10 and 19; English grammar schools typically took pupils from about 11 to 19; English Public Schools have dealt with the age-range 13 to 19; Scottish senior secondary schools ran from 12 to 18. Moreover, most children, except in the United States, tend to leave school by about sixteen, although some have further education in other institutions.

Apart from differences in age-range, some 'secondary' schooling may be simply a continuation of general education in the same school, like the German *Volksschule* or old English elementary school. Other 'secondary' schooling takes place in a distinct, purpose-built comprehensive or common school, attended by all or almost all of the children of a particular neighbourhood from the ages of eleven or twelve until they choose to leave school for work, further education, or higher education. Paradoxically, in some areas, this 'comprehensive' ideal has omitted to comprehend the practice of co-education—an interesting example of the persistence of a particular tradition in the midst of egalitarian innovation.

The process of differentiation seems to be particularly marked in secondary school learning. In the schools themselves this was traditionally reflected in the existence of separate kinds of secondary school for different groups of children (however validly or invalidly defined by social class or apparent academic aptitude). With the development of comprehensive or common secondary schools, *à la carte* principles of curriculum planning tend to supplant the few *table d'hôte* menus of separate kinds of school under the old system. Quite apart from differentiation in the schools, as children of eleven or twelve move towards being young persons of sixteen, seventeen, and eighteen, the existing differences in their talents are steadily modified and sharpened as they confront progressively more demanding problems and as they approach the necessity of choosing fairly decisively what careers they will pursue.

Compared with pre-school learning, secondary school learning is more deliberately varied and systematic—more related to community expectations and eventual vocational necessities than to personal growth within the family. In this it resembles primary school learning, except that it ranges more widely and is more directly influenced by the imminent world of work. Primary school learning trails some clouds of infant glory and has accommodated more of the ideal of personal growth and development. Secondary school learning, while usually ready to give lip service to the personal ideal, has always heard time's winged chariot hurrying near and striven to keep teen-age noses to whatever grindstone was readily available. This scholastic nose-grinding has given rise to periodical bouts of public anxiety in countries as diverse as England, France, Germany, and Russia. Compared with further or higher education, secondary school learning is less specific in its scope and purpose from the point of view of the individual learner. The engineering apprentice or college of education student knows rather more definitely what he is after. His work may be more difficult because more advanced, but it does not have the kind of breadth combined with indeterminacy that characterizes much secondary school learning.

If one were to envisage a model of the educational process from infancy to adulthood, one might think (i) of infancy as having a certain narrow unity to it, in the sense of simply growing up as a person in a particular family, (ii) of childhood from five to twelve as combining personal growth with training in a small range of the most fundamental public skills, (iii) of adolescence as a period when personal growth is challenged by a wider range of possible skills and actual social expectancies, and (iv) of late adolescence and adulthood as a period when the individual chooses his own life role (at least provisionally), trains for it, and prepares to resume something of that unified life characteristic of infancy, but at an adult level and with the sense of a wider context of life that education should have given. Whether one thinks of development from infancy to adulthood in terms of the given heredity of a particular individual, or of the social, economic, and cultural factors which sustain a rather consistent influence even in times of allegedly rapid change, or of the psychoanalytical links between infant and adult patterns of behaviour, one might conjecture that there is some common strand running through all stages of growth. To make an attempt at distinguishing particular stages of learning, either in terms of individual psychology or of learning institutions, should not cause one to ignore the possible similarities or consistencies that make the child father to the man.

Adolescent learners

It is difficult to decide whether adolescents differ markedly in character from one generation to another or whether psychologists have to keep themselves in a job by inventing new models of adolescence from generation to generation. Perhaps both factors operate, sustained by that other factor already emphasized so much in earlier chapters— the wide range of behaviour that is typically found for any human trait. If one looks at only one part of the range, whether it is for physical or academic prowess, or for delinquency or community service or anything else, one's conclusions may be supported, but have a uselessly narrow validity or applicability. The more detailed study of cultural differences among countries makes it easier to appreciate the range of adolescent behaviour—shaped by one set of norms in one place, and by another set in another place. Even within one country there may be subcultures with their separate adolescent norms, whether those of an English Public School, of a delinquent city gang, or of a young apprentices football club.

Adolescence has been pictured as a period of dramatic stress and strain. One thinks of the physiological and social pressures that thrust the young man or woman forward towards adulthood while parental restraints and other social pressures pull him or her back towards childhood Caught between opposing forces and inexperienced in resolving the complexities of a more adult world, the adolescent is imagined as enduring a period of special anxiety and vacillation. He is expected to be responsible like an adult but docile and obedient like a child. But this picture has been questioned. May it not be that adults project their own anxieties upon adolescence, as they see their children entering upon the joys of youth and repudiating the dependence of childhood? Or may it be that all stages of life have their own stresses and that the adolescent is no worse off than the middle-aged person confronted by the imminence of old age or the young child agonized by losing sixpence down a drain?

F. Musgrove in *The Educational Implications of Social and Economic Change* (Schools Council Working Paper No. 12, H.M.S.O., 1967) argues that more recent empirical studies throw a new light on adolescence. Adolescents, it is claimed, are home-centred and get on well with their parents. One of their outstanding characteristics is 'the high value they place on being natural and unaffected' (p. 55). In recent times they have lived more comfortable lives with more tolerant parents than in earlier generations. One writer is reported (p. 50) as finding that adults experienced more, not less, wishful thinking and depression than adolescents. Whatever the validity or range of applicability of such views, they represent a different picture of adolescence from what has been projected in some past writings. They underline the need to consider the time and place and representativeness of any empirical evidence purporting to validate any general view of the nature of adolescence. Circumstances may be as important as intrinsic human trends—even more important. But empirical studies themselves do not always draw attention to their own circumstantial limitations—particularly the national, regional, social, and educational contexts within which they are conducted.

Observational and experimental studies conducted by Piaget and his followers have developed the idea that adolescent intelligence is qualitatively different from earlier intelligence. The primary school child can arrange things in series and develops the power of distinguishing apparent differences from underlying identities. He is freeing himself from perceptual illusions and beginning to impose a degree of intellectual system on his world. But this progress is uneven, varying from child to child and from occasion to occasion even for the same child. Intelligence operates within the limits of concrete reference and can still be betrayed by perceptual impressions. The adolescent intelligence—roughly speaking, what Piaget calls the stage of formal operations—can handle more abstract concepts and develops into a power of thinking hypothetically about all the possible relationships among several variables, instead of about a few perceived relationships among actual objects. M. A. Wallach, observing differences of rank order among children of $1\frac{1}{2}$, 5 to 8, and 12 to 14, claims that 'whatever is being measured by "intelligence" tests is qualitatively different in infancy, early childhood, and middle childhood' (H. W. Stevenson, 1963, p. 269).

The prevailing conception of adolescent intelligence has practical importance for adolescent learning in so far as it influences learners' and teachers' notions of what is educationally feasible. Learning is influenced by the actual nature of intelligence and by ideas, whether right or wrong, about what its nature is. Suppose it were the case that intelligence, however shaped by earlier environment and however defined (ability to succeed academically, to learn quickly, to handle abstractions, to outwit rivals, to win money or favour, etc.), almost reached its peak development for any individual by mid-adolescence; then each learner's fundamental limit of intelligence would act directly on his achievements, and each teacher would accept mid-adolescent measures of intelligence as critical tokens of likely future capacity. Suppose, however, that fundamental intellectual development continued or could be significantly promoted beyond mid-adolescence (late developers, adult geniuses with third class Honours degrees) and that intelligence was a diverse rather than unified phenomenon; then learners would not necessarily hit any ceiling in mid-adolescence, or, if they hit the ceiling at one point, there would be holes in the roof for them at other points. Their teachers would take a hopeful view of the future.

Psychologists have taken diverse views of the facts about these matters. Some emphasize the limitations imposed on effective adolescent intelligence, partly by heredity and partly by ten to fifteen years' exposure to the relative consistencies of a particular social and educational environment. Others take a more optimistic view of the power of environmental modification even as late as adolescence and adulthood. Some emphasize the general intellectual factor that appears to be the substantial core of all adaptive performances. Others emphasize differences in 'conceptual tempo' (fast, slow, erratic, accurate, etc.), or in divergent-convergent thinking (*variety* of possible solutions compared with conceptual *unification*), or in the preferred kind of intellectual problem (involving objects, symbols, ideas, practical situations, etc.). Whether one speaks of 'intelligence' or 'creativity' or 'scholastic aptitude' or 'effective decision' or even substitutes test scores without words, it is impossible in practice to escape the element of social evaluation in this area. People and societies uphold their own values and put a premium on the personal qualities that are relevant to these values. Whether the empirical test is one of 'creativity' or of hunting down your next dinner in the jungle, the test is not just a measure of intrinsic individual qualities, but of such qualities in relation to social training and demand. In this sense, 'intelligence', 'creativity' and the rest are what we make them.

Today and in recent decades there have been many societies in which the demand is for more social and educational equality. This demand has naturally tended to favour theories of varied and developable abilities rather than theories of unitary 'intelligence' and relatively fixed abilities. In relation to secondary school learning this has meant an emphasis on prolonging and varying learning opportunities, to meet what are felt to be the continuing

83

and variable learning needs of young people. It is a considerable operation to work this educational ideal into the official educational system, and perhaps a still greater operation to work it into the fabric of society. Extreme traditionalists may confuse the chances of custom and inheritance with intrinsic personal merit while extreme egalitarians may confuse the desirability of fair opportunities with the achievability of equal talents or of equal status for diverse talents.

One of the outcomes of this last-mentioned ideal is a renewed concern for forms of secondary school learning quite other than traditional academic and intellectual ones. The so-called 'learning for living' ideal looks to the non-academic work which the vast majority of young people will enter, to the problems of personal, social and moral development which matter to everyone, and to the world of leisure which, in the absence of suitable education, can be the world of boredom for some. Musgrove has even proposed that 'we need a content-analysis of life in various populations defined by age, sex, occupation and life-style' (Schools Council, 1967, p. 57) as a precursor to deciding the best curriculum for secondary school learners. One cannot assume that any current life-style is necessarily a valid pattern for the future, but it is coming to be accepted that a single pattern will not meet the varied characteristics of our adolescent learners.

Of course, one cannot fit out an adolescent with a life style off the peg like a suit from a large ready-made tailor's. Acquiring an 'ego identity' is a slow and subtle business. The adolescent has to strive for such identity among a confusion of competing roles. Erikson suggests that adolescent exclusive cliques and sartorial fashions are 'a defence against a sense of identity confusion' (Erikson, 1965, p. 254). W. D. Wall suggests an adolescent need to develop a social self, a sexual self, a working self, and a 'philosophical' self in the sense of a self with some general
84

attitude to life however vaguely or precisely formulated (W. F. Connell, 1967, p. 258). The adolescent peer-group or peer-culture has sometimes been represented as an important shaper of adolescent attitudes, but some have questioned this (Schools Council, 1967, p. 51), arguing that adolescents share many of their parents' main attitudes. A full statement of the truth would probably embrace both points of view. Parents have had ten to fifteen years in which to influence their children before any adolescent peer-culture begins to operate. At the same time, the peer-group does offer a useful half-way house to adult independence, a forum for personal experimentation or exploration along with those sharing similar problems at a particular stage of life.

Wall has summed up adolescence very neatly in his assertion that:

the purely maturational aspects are difficult to distinguish and the content and direction of growth are much more determined by prior experiences in childhood, by the attitudes and expectations of adults and by the general climate of the community in which the youth finds himself (W. F. Connell, 1967, p. 256).

This is illustrated in a 1953 comparison of the adolescent attitudes of children in grammar schools and secondary modern schools (Schools Council, 1967, p. 15). The latter communicated less easily with parents and were less sure of parental approval, they had lower aspirations, they preferred security and routine to interest and independence, they were less involved in school life, and they tended to be more dogmatic. Himmelweit, the author of this part of the Schools Council's twelfth Working Paper, saw the most urgent educational need of such children as being that of learning to communicate and to express thought about problems meaningful to young people.

85

The material of adolescent learning

In the minds of some, 'material' perhaps refers to the
adolescents themselves—the 'stuff' that is squeezed through
the scholastic sausage machine—but this is not what is
intended here. The question is, What do or should adolescents learn? Much of what they learn—and learn most
deeply—is learned from family and social circumstances
rather than scholastic curricula. There are lessons in
wealth and poverty, in rejection and affection, in selfish-
ness and altruism, in concern and indifference, in hope-
fulness and dejection, in resignation and ambition—all
arising from the particular family, society, and educational
system with which a young person grows up. These
environmental factors powerfully modify behaviour, attitudes, and identifications. They shape them both by acting
directly on the young and by determining the status of the
schools' particular contribution to such shaping.

So long as success in an academic curriculum has been
the touchstone of adolescent schooling—and it perhaps
still is; or even, in a sense, must be in a highly developed
society—most young people have been obliged to find their
effective education (apart from the simple scholastic skills)
in their families and local societies rather than in their
schools. Many even of the ablest, when admitted to grammar schools, have been acutely aware of the gap between
school culture and family culture. The great majority of
people in the middle or lower ranges of academic ability
have found still less possibility of identifying themselves
with the (to them) alien world of scholastic and intellectual values. Egalitarian thinkers have attacked this problem in various ways—at one time concentrating on
scholastic opportunities for the ablest working-class children; then campaigning for a common schooling for all
(which has a diversity of possible interpretations); and
sometimes trying either to deflate traditional culture

(representing it perhaps as simply the folk-ways of a dominant minority) or to inflate popular culture (representing it as having as much value for those who belong to or appreciate it as Shakespeare, Bach, or Picasso for the highbrows).

Egalitarianism flows along one channel into making the material of learning (in a wide sense) more similar for everyone, and along another channel into making the material of learning more diverse. Unification of the organizational structure of education is meant to reduce inequalities of status and opportunity. Diversification of educational courses within the structure is meant to give equal if different opportunities within the whole range of studies available. Such a programme still needs to be matched by parallel developments in other aspects of society. One can appreciate how difficult this is when one considers how slow various countries have been to add a year to the *minimal* school-leaving age (which, incidentally, may be called simply the school-leaving age, or still more discouragingly, the *compulsory* school-leaving age). Minimal school-leaving ages, different kinds of school structure, different social backgrounds, different attitudes to culture and society—these may not be what is ordinarily meant by the material of learning, but they still may be the *very* material of learning.

Whether adolescents are thrust outside the pale of 'real' academic education or whether they are impounded within it (which fate is worse?), they might all benefit from more opportunities of informal discussion of the personal problems of adolescent and adult life—problems about work, marriage, philosophies of life, the fruitful use of leisure, and so on. Even those most favoured in family background and scholastic opportunity have often carried remarkable areas of ignorance and confusion forward into adult life. Those less favoured may suffer, in addition, from lack of opportunity and training in even *expressing* their ignor-

87

ance and confusion, and, therefore, are less likely to have chances of dispelling either.

Writers on education have campaigned for a long time for more attention to be given to education in matters that are of felt concern to young people, but, while there have been changes, the policy is not as simple to operate as it might seem. Attitudes on important problems are more naturally (whether rightly or wrongly) shaped in the family over long periods than in comparatively large school classes over quite short periods. Where educational counselling and guidance have flourished, as in the United States, for a long time, there is probably still a tension with traditional academic values. And, third, academic skills (mathematical and scientific understanding, ability to write logically in clear English, understanding the background of the social and personal problems arising in communities) are intrinsically of vital practical importance, even if they carry accretions of scholastic junk.

P. H. Hirst has suggested the importance of distinguishing educational objectives, educational content, and educational methods (Schools Council, 1967, p. 74). The objectives he proposes are [i] 'an attitude of critical questioning, a more exploratory approach to solving the practical problems of everyday life, an open attitude to social change, a desire to take decisions on rational grounds, and so on'; [ii] 'to hand on explicitly a body of social and moral values'; [iii] 'an understanding of the institutions of our society and of social and personal relationships'; [iv] 'the mastery of a whole battery of social and practical skills that are important in contemporary society'; and [v] the presentation of new developments in traditional areas of knowledge. Although Hirst did not feel that there was any extensive empirical evidence of how best to organize content and methods so as to achieve these objectives, he stresses the importance of an active role for the teacher 'now that we recognize that the development of mind is centrally dependent on socially acquired conceptual schemes, critical attitudes, principles, etc.' (p. 82).

The material of adolescent learning was perhaps easier to define when almost the sole objective was the mastery of the Latin language, although schools were always expected to do something about moral or religious objectives at least incidentally. Between the eighteenth and twentieth centuries the Latin curriculum very slowly and reluctantly broadened out into a wider range of studies, including modern languages, science, and the other staple ingredients of a general academic education in the twentieth century. Even this breadth was found too narrow and too distantly related to 'life'. Schools in the United States have long offered a more variegated curriculum to many of their adolescent pupils, just as other countries must as they slowly extend and prolong compulsory or customary secondary education as it has been extended and prolonged in the States. This trend postpones the decisive evaluation of individual talents, but, sooner or later, societies put their own price tags on different talents in one way or another. All knowledge is not judged of equal worth.

This is not the place to develop the theme of curriculum planning. Enough has been said to remind the student of adolescent learning that there is considerable competition both among the actual learning materials proffered deliberately or accidentally to adolescents and among the kinds of learning material that are commended as suitable for their supposed needs. Both in practice and in policy there has been a persisting spirit of revisionism, in the direction of relating the curriculum more closely to 'life' —if one could only determine what 'life' is or ought to be.

Institutions of adolescent learning

It is not by chance that this chapter began with a reference to the institutional aspect of secondary school learning, for most of the problems arise from the clash between various strong institutional traditions and an egalitarian revisionist reaction against them. Several aspects of this tension have already been mentioned and a full study of it could be a life's work in comparative education. Fortunately, it is possible to state briefly some of the main institutional aspects of secondary school learning, and the most important may be the comparative recency of the idea of secondary education for all as a practical policy. Indeed, the idea of secondary education for anyone is not yet very old, for the word 'secondary' only comes into use when there is a public education system, divided into separate stages.

Until this century there was no question of a prolonged education for any but a small minority of children. Even when state elementary education developed in the nineteenth century this was a separate and inferior kind of education and continued to be so well into the twentieth century. The fortunate minority—mainly fortunate by wealth and social status, but with loopholes for able children from less favoured homes—received a grammar school type of education as their main formal education, with preparatory schooling serving the subordinate function which its title suggests. This was so whether the school was called grammar school, public school, *Gymnasium*, *lycée*, high school, academy, or any other such title. The recruitment to such schools, the aims, curricula and methods, and the careers to which they led, were all upheld by long scholastic traditions and by the established pattern of society itself. Most children were educationally and socially outside this academic tradition and entered the world of work in early adolescence or earlier still. Most children still are outside this tradition and enter the world of work by 15 or 16, while their academic brethren continue to be schooled for several or many years.

During the twentieth century new institutions have been created. In some countries the nineteenth-century elementary school kept slowly growing at the top so that the senior classes were doing some work which might now be done in a separate secondary school. The German *Volksschule*, providing most German children with their whole general education, is still something like this—partly like the English all-age schools which completely disappeared only surprisingly recently. Where countries departed from the *Volksschule* idea and sought separate secondary schools for all, general secondary schools were sometimes established, with less academic emphasis than in the grammar school type. English secondary modern and Scottish junior secondary schools were examples of this, although also examples of how similar institutions can differ, for, while *some* secondary modern schools admitted 85 to 90 per cent of an age group (and included, therefore, some quite academic children) Scottish junior secondary schools typically lacked any recruits from the top 25 to 30 per cent of the academic ability range.

The next institutional development was the common or comprehensive secondary school. The name has been applied to quite different kinds of school. In its most egalitarian version it might be a purpose-built school, admitting almost the whole range of adolescent abilities, postponing differentiated curricula for several years, and deliberately putting children of diverse abilities and backgrounds in the same class. Actual schools may approximate to these criteria, but they may be far from being purpose-built or even well adapted, they may lack whole ranges of pupils (for example, through recruiting from a homogeneous neighbourhood, or excluding all children of a particular sex, or having to compete with fee-paying private schools), and they may differentiate pupils and courses from the start.

Scottish secondary schools—particularly those in small

towns—have claimed to be comprehensive for decades or even centuries. Some have certainly admitted all of the children of secondary school age in their districts, but the prevailing atmosphere was traditional and academic. They had some of the modern comprehensive ideal in at least educating everyone more or less together, and in holding out the academic ideal (still highly prized by society) to everyone, but they would not have satisfied the more enthusiastic 'comprehensive' ideologists of more recent times. Comprehensive education will continue to mean very different things, if only because of architectural and regional variations, the high cost of achieving anything nearer uniformity, and the power of national or local custom (illustrated in the matter of coeducation).

So long as most children leave school at fifteen or sixteen many must depend for their further education on institutions other than secondary schools—technical colleges, industrial training schemes, and so on. The Crowther Report of 1959 made clear how deficient English provision for further education continued to be. After the war of 1914-18 and again after the 1939-45 war there was ineffectual legislation to strengthen further education. The more recent Industrial Training Act represents another legislative attack on part of the problem. It takes a universal state system of some kind (and possibly a certain level of general socio-cultural development as well) to enforce universal educational standards. Without some such general sanctions, employers and employees tend to do what suits their immediate interests rather than what may benefit even their own longer-term material interests, not to mention other personal or community interests. Confronted with any question about the institutional contribution to adolescent learning, one would have to attach great importance to the improvement of further education. Despite the snags already mentioned, it probably has its own advantages in so far as it helps the adolescent forward into the adult world rather than (as he may feel it) keeping him back in the world of childhood and school.

There are, of course, many informal or semi-formal institutions which may contribute significantly to the learning of at least some adolescents—youth organizations of various kinds, clubs, choirs, sports teams, Outward Bound groups, and so on. Very many adolescents are hardly touched by any of the semi-formal youth institutions, but, for large numbers, leisure institutions of one kind or another may establish life-long interests and allegiances of a valuable and constructive kind. In terms of lasting valuable change, such institutions can produce as much learning as formal schooling, although those who draw most benefit from either may tend to draw most from both.

Methods of teaching and learning in secondary schools

Secondary schools have tended to be more resistant to changing their methods than primary schools—partly because of the institutional factors outlined in the preceding section, partly because of subject specialization and the difficulty of combining parallel specialist teaching programmes into a coherent educative force. The experimental study that most readily comes to mind as matching Gardner's work in primary schools is the 'Eight-Year Study' carried out with 1475 matched pairs of students in thirty United States high schools during the nineteen-thirties. The general conclusion was that the students in the 'progressive' schools did at least as well academically as those in traditional schools and showed up even better on assessments of intellectual curiosity, aesthetic appreciation, resourcefulness in new situations, concern about world affairs, and some other general characteristics like these. (W. M. Aiken, 1942, *The Story of the Eight-Year Study*, New York, Harper.)

Such evidence from the progressivist camp has not perhaps convinced many traditionalists, but rather comforted those who were inclined in any case to favour less rigid teaching and learning methods. However, the gradual extension of the period of secondary schooling, the increase in the proportion staying beyond the minimal leaving age, and the efforts (already described) of egalitarian and learning-for-life reformers, have combined to loosen up some of the old rigidities of secondary schooling—the talk and chalk, the scholastic grind, the dictated notes, the ploys to hoodwink examiners but bowing of necks to the examiners' yoke all the same. Not that these have vanished by any means—they have impressive staying power. Nor does their vanishing necessarily herald a progressivist dawn —but sometimes only a demoralizing lack of purpose. But more schools are becoming sensitive to the arguments of the Newsom Report, which are applicable to more than the children of average ability specifically designated. In particular, adolescents should be given more choice and responsibility, be treated more like adults than children even if they are neither, and be taught in more informal and participating ways instead of sitting in stiff rows not listening to lectures on topics which are not seen to be significant for them.

V. S. Krutesky and N. S. Lukin in their discussion of 'Self Discipline in Adolescents' (Redl, 1964, pp. 22-44) make some interesting points about adolescent education in Russian society. They naturally think of discipline as signifying obedience and responsibility within the framework of Soviet society. 'True discipline,' they say, 'is composed of various relationships in a collective' and should be a conscious process of self-discipline. Adolescents should have a well-organized work programme and their self-respect should be sustained, partly by not injuring their natural sensitivity. Teachers should develop a sense of right tone and timing. They should keep cool, be consistent, adhere to promises, admit faults (but not have too many), be ready to forgive and forget group misdemeanours, uphold expectations of improvement, occasionally joke or turn a blind eye, and rarely show anger. Perhaps a counsel of perfection, but still worth heeding!

The idea of discipline through 'relationships in a collective' may not appeal to non-communist educators, and yet something rather like it has partly characterized some of our most influential schools (the Public schools, for example). And where secondary education has been weakest, as in *some* secondary modern schools, it is partly because of the lack of a strong collective factor. Pupils leave early, teachers do not stay long, families expect their children to become wage-earners as soon as possible, society has time only for the academically and socially successful, and generally, the parts of the enterprise just do not support one another. Hence the campaign for school reorganization in the hope of at least partly modifying maleficent features of the old structure.

Examinations notoriously tend to cast a dark shadow over secondary school teaching. And while many people deplore the shadow, they seem to have great difficulty in dispelling it. A kind of love-hate relationship develops— 'loving' the system for its compulsive motivation and for the possibility of chalking up successes on the public scoreboard, hating it for its mechanical drudgery and the tyranny of the examining bodies. Teaching for examinations is an art in itself. The teachers sometimes almost take the examinations vicariously by their dictated notes and coaching in examination techniques. Teaching may come to be dominated by considerations of prestige in the examinations race, with wider educational considerations neglected. And, while the system may be condemned, the threat of freedom from external examining may be still more terrifying for some, for this implies a more self-motivating learning system and more local responsibility for setting standards.

95

Such local autonomy can obviously have a liberating effect on teaching and learning, but, the wider the expected currency of any scholastic award the more necessary the creation of a device for upholding its status. Such a device may consist of a regional or national examining board, but that takes one away from local autonomy and has its own problems of reliable and valid examining. It may consist of an informal moderator or group of moderators, keeping a helpful eye on local standards without over-determining the learning programme. It may consist of objective tests (where such exist) with which local achievements can be compared, giving at least one wider reference point for local assessors. It may consist of an accreditation scheme such as is used in some countries to validate the general educational standards of a school or college. It may consist of a strengthening of professional standards so that no one is inclined to question the assessment of any properly qualified member of the profession—although this is difficult in a profession so diverse as teaching. But, however pupil assessment is arranged or standards sanctioned, these arrangements and standards become almost intrinsic features of the learning and teaching situation. They tend to determine, with more latitude or less, what is learned and taught and in what manner.

Given the curricula and examinations typical of traditional academic secondary schools (grammar school, *lycée*, *Gymnasium*, etc.), and even with the rather select, educationally favoured group of adolescents traditionally enrolled in such schools, much of the teaching and learning had the defects, already mentioned, of contrived and temporary achievements—often in skills which the pupils had no genuine interest in acquiring (literary 'appreciation', translation into or out of Latin, memorization of mathematical theorems or historical compendia). Teaching has been conducted in the expository mode, with considerable stress on mnemonic aids to reproduction of whatever formulae seem likely to win marks in examinations. That is the black side. It has seemed blacker as a wider range of abilities becomes represented in common secondary schools. If the old formula did not suit even all of the small group exposed to it in less egalitarian days, how can it suit a much larger group and a different kind of society?

There have been strong movements for the reform of curricula, assessments, and learning methods to meet the apparent needs of a wider spectrum of adolescent learners. Such reform, although tending to be inspired by the problems of less academically orientated children, *could* be beneficial to the academic as well, by bringing their studies into closer relationship with the facts of adolescent life and of modern society. At this stage, the '*could*' has to be underlined, for we do not know whether some of the features of the bad old days may be necessary or advantageous for the training of the intellectually ablest. For example, it might be that an institution, like a grammar school, concentrating its efforts unquestioningly on a particular range of values and achievements tends to uphold these values and achievements more strongly than an institution, such as a comprehensive school, where loyalties are more diverse and efforts more dissipated.

It is not too easy to settle the empirical question of whether this is true or not, for it is a complex matter to assess. It is no easier to settle the question of principle as to the relative importance for a society of training an intellectual élite (scientific, technological, etc.) and of training other groups. 'Democracies' as diverse as the United States and the Soviet Union make very specific provision for élitist training. England, France and Germany have been slow to modify powerful élitist traditions in secondary education. In all of these countries, teaching and learning by traditional exposition, verbal systematization, memorization, exercise, and examination persist to an impressive extent, despite all the writings and activities of 'reformers'. Even if one wishes to cast down or modify an established élite, it is still necessary to train a new one. And, if the old academic learning methods have their faults, they may (particularly in modernized versions) accord as well with the academic skills required as learning methods ('integrated curriculum', 'projects', etc.) designed for elementary education or less academic secondary programmes. Briefly, chalk-and-talk and paper-and-pencil may have more validity for some purposes than for others. We do not have decisive evidence on these questions.

Despite the possible defensibility of some traditional teaching and learning methods and the dearth of decisive evidence about specific practices, there is at least a certain plausibility about some of the newer analyses of secondary school teaching and learning. Much important, and even quite technical learning (child-rearing, cooking, tax-form-returning, etc.) is acquired *en route* through necessary activity in response to situations which matter to the learner, and is examined not by examination paper but by problem situations themselves as they arise. Would it not be sensible to organize school learning on similar lines, even if the problem situations have to be engineered in the form of projects, visits, practical activities of all kinds? Such learning could be life-like in specific aims and in methods of pursuing them. Since adolescents have to prepare to some extent for problems that may be imminent but not already there, teachers obviously must create programmes of activity and study that foreshadow the problems of young adult working life. This ideal has been successfully acted on in many schools, but, to be realistic, one must recognize that it has many problems. Without mustering detailed evidence of this, the example might be mentioned of communist countries which have long experimented with work-orientated programmes of adolescent education, and in societies where one would have judged circumstances favourable to the arrangement, but which have, nonetheless, run into considerable practical difficulties—to the extent of modifying the programmes back towards greater school-centredness at certain periods.

Secondary schooling is so diverse that it is difficult to find common ground for discussion, even among teachers within one country—sometimes even among teachers within one type of school within one country, because of regional and individual idiosyncracies. What might one find in an imaginary school which embodied all of the most admirable policies for effective secondary school learning? It had better be in a socially mixed neighbourhood, so that the egalitarians are satisfied. Alternatively, one might have it in an urban slum area but give the school such a high educational reputation (excellent staff, facilities, etc.) that well-to-do parents would fight tooth and nail to get their children into it. If it is in England, then one will imagine the Public Schools closed—just to keep these parents keenly interested.

This school will be a very good comprehensive school. That is, it will have all the material, organizational, and human facilities that a 'comprehensivist' would want in his ideal school. There is a large sixth form and the academically inclined sixth-formers get all that they would have got from an old grammar school, plus a sense of community with the diversity of non-academically inclined pupils with whom they have shared classes in the lower school. A great deal of incidental learning goes on in connection with a huge range of clubs, societies, and general school activities—catering for specialized interests and talents, or bringing specialists together in common musical, sporting, or other interests. This kind of learning is considered an integral part of the school's 'teaching' effort; it is not an indulgence remote from the serious work of examination-grinding. The school's educational and vocational counselling service operates a continuous programme which helps each individual to channel himself in accordance with his abilities, interests, and circumstances into the best set of studies for him. Time-tables had better be computerized.

The whole emphasis of the school is on each learner building up a programme of work that will develop his sense of achievement and pride in personal growth. The work is based on individual or group investigations and exercises, but there is no assumption that such work will generate itself out of the blue. There is a considerable element of fairly traditional learning—a kind of parallel support programme of essential fundamentals for all and special programmes according to subsequently developing interests and capacities. Those who want to take any examinations do so in a business-like way, but with no build-up of examination fever—no special acclaim for success or reproach for failure. School reports on achievement are made in an honest but positive spirit and employers welcome these as much as examination successes. Where examination successes are required by outside bodies, these are worked for soberly but without panic.

The tone set by teachers and parents, the guidance programme, the material facilities (audio-visual aids, musical instruments, sports equipment, libraries, etc.), the social life of the school, the habit of individual and group work, the no-fuss-no-nonsense approach to examinations, the adolescent-centred, life-centred, and yet tradition-enriched curricula and syllabuses, the emphasis on learning through pupil activity with teacher guidance—these *are* the teaching and learning methods. Things like television and other audio-visual aids, programmed learning, team-teaching, out-of-school visits, and other comparable devices are just incidentals—used as readily as a traditional teacher would pick up the chalk or tell the pupils to open jotters. They are important, but subsidiary to the teaching and learning principles embodied in the very structure and atmosphere of the school as an institution.

At this point one had better call a halt. The 'idealist' will be intoxicated by such a vision and the 'realist' enraged by it. It was an attempt to clear aside possible organizational reforms of secondary schooling so that one might isolate teaching and learning methods as such. But, with secondary schooling, such methods are almost inextricably mixed up with questions of what the curriculum and organization should be—not only what is desirable, but what is feasible, given a teaching profession which cannot reasonably be expected to conform 100 per cent to the idyll just outlined, a society which may be unable to give the necessary support to the values and practices described through not itself really subscribing to them, and parents who may put before any such balanced educational values an absolute priority demand for sheer academic and vocational advancement, or, alternatively, for withdrawal of their children from the 'unreal' world of school at the earliest opportunity.

Reform of teaching and learning methods is not just a technical exercise for the teaching profession. It is a major operation of getting school and society to agree upon curricula, syllabuses, and experimental attitudes which will bring more closely together the realities of what teachers can attempt (let alone achieve) with given scholastic and social resources, and the realities of the cultural inheritance which is, in a sense, objectively there for any young people who choose to take possession of at least part of it.

Perspective on secondary school learning

It is no easy matter to achieve a perspective on adolescent learning—that formal and informal learning which takes place during the years of secondary schooling or further education but not, of course, only or even mainly within the institutional framework of such schooling or education. Such a perspective has to take in the variety among individuals, whole societies, social groups within a society, past and present scholastic institutions, educational and social values and aspirations, psychological characteristics at different periods of the life-span, social fashions in different generations or even at different times within one generation, educational methods, material provisions, family attitudes to schooling, and modes of preparing for the teaching profession. Any single one of these variables can provoke hot disputation—between different generations, different school traditions, different national, social or cultural classes. Adolescent learning is likely to go on being a very lively topic.

The period of adolescence is something of a battleground for conflicting adult interests, striving to win the young for egalitarianism or for traditional class values, for the arts or sciences or particular mixtures of both, for prolonged education or speedy earning, for altruistic social endeavour or effective self-advancement, for materialism or humanism or religion. The 'teen-age culture' itself, with its varying conformities of dress, music, dancing, and social gathering, is to some extent a product of commercial management, although still a reflection of what may be a perennial, maturational urge for action and stimulation among people of one's own age—an urge that may exist and be commercially exploited at all ages, but draw particular attention to itself in adolescence because of the sheer exuberance and vitality of youth.

When one considers how relatively short the period of secondary schooling is for most adolescents in most European countries, one can understand a certain hesitation, or even panic, about the idea of trying to change substantially the educational shaping of the dozen years' upbringing and schooling before adolescence. It is easier to accept broad individual expectations as they are at twelve rather than to think of creating new self-images for those with limited achievements and hopes. It is easier to accept established institutions of secondary and further education, with their traditional curricula, methods, and atmospheres, than to experiment with laborious, costly, and unproven reforms which might (or might not) give new chances to the old 'failures' and a better education to the old 'academically successful'. Individual reforming teachers or schools demonstrate that various reforms can work (for them), but this does not always convince the mass of teachers and schools, or produce very rapid or widespread change towards a new educational ideal. The ideal will be branded as 'all very well in theory', unless it is boosted through substantial political, social, or financial support from the community as a whole.

Some reformers have tried to get out of this impasse. By combined national and local enquiries into practical ways of reforming curricula and methods, it may be possible to achieve broad agreement on reforms that are desirable and practicable, but also to adapt such reforms to fit varying local circumstances. National and local committees of teachers and others concerned with schooling can provide mutual nourishment—not surrendering ideals because of difficulties, but still taking account of practical difficulties in particular interpretations of any general ideal. The operations of the Schools Council in England illustrate something of this pattern. It is bound to have its own problems, for competing interests persist even if they are brought to the conference table, but it does seem to offer some hope of a way forward—especially if considered along with other special research and development programmes in individual branches of education, such as the sciences, mathematics, or the humanities.

Another major route out of the impasse runs through in-service programmes for teachers. Until quite recently, a teacher's professional preparation—whether it consisted of university study or teacher-training or both—was expected to last him for almost half a century. When combined with the conservatism of schools themselves as institutions (buildings and books too costly to replace, work patterns too laborious to change, etc.), the pattern of professional preparation kept much education well and truly stuck in its frozen rut. More teachers can now expect to refresh themselves intellectually and professionally by organized courses of further study and practical work as well as by participation in local and national trials of new curricula, syllabuses and methods.

Educational administrators, locally and nationally, have become more concerned with the possibilities of speeding up educational developments by positive intervention and planning. *Laissez-faire* does not get results on a big scale. Dogmatic, centralized planning without the active participation of localities and individuals may achieve a certain uniformity of standard, but not the flexibility and subtlety of interpretation that depend on extensive individual commitment to programmes of reform. Training in, and experience of, active innovation have to be created and developed if the gap between ideal and practice is to be narrowed. This, in turn, requires analysis in economic and educational terms of the potentiality of various educational programmes. Text-books, audio-visual aids, learning machines, curricula, and syllabuses have to be weighed up in more critical detail to determine what gives the best educational value for the money spent on education.

This apparently, and to some extent genuinely, more rational approach to educational planning is likely to create new problems as well as solve some of the old ones. For example, the ideal of harmonizing local and national endeavours is difficult to achieve. The more powerful, and within its own limits more effective, a centralized body is, the more does it tend to attract human and material resources to itself, to detract (even if unintentionally) from regional and local resources, and to undervalue regional and local values and circumstances. This is constantly illustrated in metropolitan attitudes, which can be as narrowly blinkered as those of a remote village. The importance of this for secondary school learning is that the teachers who carry out the educational programmes in the schools can become second-class citizens in the educational world. The people who count most in terms of direct impact upon children may count least in a wider educational world where politicians, economists, and sociologists presume to lay down the educational law.

In a highly developed system of education like that in the United States, which the English system increasingly tends to resemble, actual school-teaching is only a step towards educational administration or college-teaching for the most able and ambitious men who deign to become teachers at all. This underlines the earlier suggestion that, as educational opportunity becomes 'more equal' at the secondary level, the education that decides career and life patterns moves higher up the educational ladder. The egalitarian line of battle moves from equal secondary opportunity for all to equal tertiary opportunity for all. And in the United States one third of all young people do go to college—to a college of *some* kind.

Despite these problems about planning and the fact that sheer defectiveness of material resources is one of the major limitations on educational endeavour, individual schools and individual teachers still have considerable power of action. They have available to them today a superior understanding of the psychology and sociology of adolescence, of the nature of secondary schools as institutional forces, of the possibilities of evolving new curricula and methods more closely related to adolescent life and modern society, of the value of extra-scholastic institutions in educating young people. In and out of school they can develop in their pupils humane, useful, and lively activities and interests which, in the worst possible circumstances, offer a glimmer of light to the socially or educationally handicapped and, in average circumstances, rescue a good deal of the total educational endeavour from complete subservience to defective community values.

It may be that the development of further education in all its variety is an important key to the general improvement of adolescent learning. It could extend a tertiary educational aspiration to all adolescents and offer a possibility of reinforcing secondary school studies by linking them with further education programmes. But this is a rather vague hope at present. The necessary institutions and training programmes for their teachers have a long way to go. In the meantime, secondary schools must do the best they can to provide their own reinforcement for adolescent learning. Hitherto there have been large numbers of adolescents who have simply not felt that school learning was worth their while, and—perhaps a more serious obstacle—large numbers of parents who have shared their children's view. Possibilities of changing parental views are being studied, but these, in their turn, are often powerfully shaped by particular experiences of society. Policies for housing, employment, and the like, might then be stronger arguments than any verbal exhortations about the value of education.

5

Some learning problems

Developmental perspective

It was suggested towards the end of the first chapter that
learning is a controversial topic and that there is no justification for assuming that the analysis of learning should
ever be strikingly simple or non-technical. And at the beginning of the third chapter a dozen considerations were
listed that may be helpful in analysing learning problems.
The preceding four chapters, taken together, offer a developmental perspective on learning. They point out features
of learning at different educational stages of a person's
career, distinguishing one stage from another up to a point,
but also outlining characteristics and means of analysing
them that are relevant to all stages. This last chapter is
mainly concerned to suggest further possible lines of
enquiry.

Theory and practice

Those in the middle of a practical learning situation,
whether as learners themselves or as teachers, are under-
standably impatient to know the specific answers to their
own specific problems. They tend to want directly applicable formulae rather than general understanding. The latter
may guide decision and action but only at the cost of

continual and subtle interpretative effort. It is, in one sense, easier to be told what to do, whether through a prescribed syllabus, a headmasterly fiat, a standard text, or an external examination. But those fortunate enough to be able to study learning as a whole are bound to see that the map is an intricate one, not inviting many simple unqualified directives.

These differing standpoints and perspectives have often created an unfortunate barrier between 'theorists' and 'practitioners'. One must use inverted commas, for it would be naïve to suppose that the 'practitioner' is not assuming some theory or that the 'theorist'—even the 'pure theorist' —will not have at least certain attitudes towards practice. That some on both sides are prepared to be naïve about this indicates an emotional problem which could be helped by more frequent expressions of mutual sympathy, less frequent back-biting, and more readiness to distinguish different learning problems, for the disputants in this kind of situation are often talking about different things while pretending that they are the same.

The word 'theory' itself is a stumbling block. Some give it a weak meaning (for example, 'a speculative view') and then dismiss some account or proposal as 'mere theory'. Some give it a strong meaning (for example, 'a systematic body of principles which economically explain a set of phenomena and which have withstood systematic attempts to disprove them') and then question any lesser account as being 'not a real theory'. But there are defensible intermediate senses of 'theory', for example, a version of the strong meaning which allows for the difference, *in degree of precision at the very least*, between the physical and social sciences. And there is 'theory' in the sense of 'theory of value', meaning a reasoned view of values or logical analysis of value judgements. A 'theory of education' means a theory of values and a theory of how they can be achieved.

'Learning theory' and personal interaction

'Learning theory' has come to be applied in a narrow technical sense to the academic products of certain neo-behaviourist psychologists, some of whom would disclaim any relevance of their work to classroom learning. Two lucid approaches to this experimental, behaviourist analysis of learning are provided by W. F. Hill's *Learning, A Survey of Psychological Interpretations* and D. E. Broadbent's *Behaviour*, while M. L. Bigge in his *Learning Theories for Teachers* perhaps defies the notion that learning theory has little or no connection with ordinary learning. It is not possible to discuss 'learning theory' in this special sense within the limits of the present book, although the discussion of behaviourism in chapters 1 and 2 offered a starting point and the topic can become absorbing for those who are sympathetic to experiment, systematization and attempted precision.

A contrasting approach and attitude is represented in E. Richardson's *The Environment of Learning* (and, in a more limited context, in her *Group Study for Teachers*). This takes one more immediately into human learning situations and has more affinities with the psychoanalytic than with the behaviourist analysis of phenomena. General students of learning may find the emphasis on interpersonal relationships and feelings more directly intelligible and relevant than the learning theorists' schematizations. But this has its problems too, for, in addition to the necessity of accepting the limitations of a clinical-descriptive analysis, one is invited and challenged to look at aspects of the learning situation which may create their own apprehensions—the currents of feeling that transfuse apparently neutral or scholastic exchanges, the ulterior uses of human relationships (cf. Berne's *Games People Play*), and the changing patterns of behaviour in groups ('group dynamics') which may almost show a life of their own despite their derivation from individual behaviour.

This is an interesting and fruitful approach to learning in itself, but it can yield further interest and illumination if contrasted with the writings of the 'learning theorists' or, in another direction, with the ecological approach of Lorenz, for example, in his book *On Aggression*. The interpersonal approach, if it may be so described for brevity, also raises questions of how far learning is a kind of therapeutic process and how far a process of acquiring skills, and of how much these two overlap. The answers may be complex, for some learning is obviously facilitated by sympathetic emotional involvement (learning to share at least some of the loved one's tastes) while other learning takes place despite emotional disincentives (learning to put up with various painful situations). Moreover, an interpersonal analysis of the kind illustrated in Miss Richardson's writings might be compared with the different kind of interpersonal analysis represented in a book such as Argyle's *The Psychology of Interpersonal Behaviour*.

Learning and motivation

This is a theme that always appeals to those engaged in learning or teaching. How does one motivate oneself or others to learn what has to be learned? The answer is that motivation is not so simple a concept as the question may suggest. The question seems to invite advice about pushing the right buttons, whereas learners are not machines with buttons to press. R. S. Peters in *The Concept of Motivation* has stressed certain differences between men and the rest of nature—particularly that men understand some of the laws in accordance with which they act and, in addition, 'act in accordance with a quite different set of laws —normative laws—which they themselves create' (Peters, 1960, p. 97). Learning implies reaching some norm or standard that men have proposed for themselves. Men act in accordance with rules proposed by themselves; they are not just moved by hypothetical 'drives' or 'needs'. 'Need' itself, as has frequently been pointed out but persistently ignored, is a normative concept, always assuming some goal to be desirable, even if it is the humble goal of survival.

In practical terms, the problem of motivation is that of presenting particular learning goals that are sufficiently closely related to the capacities of the individual learner in circumstances which facilitate the learner's attaining the goals. Practical motivation is, therefore, quite a complex matter of learning about individual differences, and setting attainable rather than unattainable goals, and assessing which circumstances are fixed (at least for the present) and which can be manipulated to encourage learning. It is a matter of studying all the things that have been discussed in earlier chapters of this book and following up those aspects or stages of learning which one is concerned to control. Not that one has to do this all for oneself, for much of the practical knowledge about such things is already embodied in learning institutions. The purpose of deliberate study is to extend one's understanding of what others already know and to find possibilities of improvement upon existing achievements.

The emphasis throughout this book has been on the variety of factors that are relevant to an understanding of learning and, therefore, of motivation to learning. It is not just a matter of the psychology of learning but of the sociology of learning, and not only in the sense of a few social factors currently impinging upon learning but in the sense of the inheritance of cultural and scholastic institutions and values which set the context for any discussion of learning. Highly particular problems such as how to get little Johnny to bother about literary sensitivity or moral rectitude must be related to such questions as whether little Johnny's society bothers about them any more than he does. Perhaps the typical teacher's frustration lies in recognizing more circumstances that are beyond his control than are within it. The answer sometimes is to change the immediate goal to bring it within the area of what is practicable.

Structure in learning

The question of manipulating goals and circumstances leads naturally to the question of structure in learning. As people have come to understand more of the variables affecting learning—the kinds of variable discussed throughout this book—they have also begun to speculate about and experiment with more radical restructuring of many learning situations. If traditional school buildings almost impose talk-and-chalk teaching and discourage change, then one chooses a new building with variable spaces designed to stimulate more varied and active patterns of learning. Class sets of a single text-book may be replaced, where appropriate, by fewer copies of a larger variety of books. Time-tables may be less rigidly divided up on arithmetical principles and more flexibly related to the requirements of different kinds of activity and different kinds of pupil. Carefully graded programmes of concrete experience and experimentation may be devised to underpin more abstract verbal and numerical skills. Total prescription of curriculum or syllabus may be modified to give learners opportunities of choice. School and class organization may be changed, as in the introduction of mixed ability classes or comprehensive schools.

The reader can extend these examples for himself, perhaps classifying structural changes in terms of diverse factors—internal administration, local or national policy, syllabus or curriculum, social environment, professional training, general psychological principles, and, no doubt, others. The point of general importance is that there are many factors to be manipulated, and that a few at least of the barriers to manipulating them are barriers in people's own minds. They may simply not see the freedom that they could exercise. This is not necessarily a matter for reproach, for a sense of imprisonment felt in the ranks of a profession often springs from a sense of imprisonment long imposed upon the profession.

There are other reasons for slowness in making decisive structural change. Not all change is for the better and different groups in a community give allegiance to different values. Even where there is no fundamental dispute about values, there is often failure to support agreed policies with sufficient material resources. And even when material resources are adequate, there may be failure to give weight to regional differences or to appreciate the motivational gap between the person who is a prime mover and another who feels himself just a pawn in the game. There is an increasing appreciation of the need to make explicit systematic provision for opportunities of reviewing attitudes and sharpening skills at every level of the educational enterprise, but financial stringency does not sweeten the pill of rapid innovation.

Despite what has just been said, the structure of learning can be considered at a more personal level, disregarding material and organizational rigidities. Whether concerned with one's own learning problems or (as a teacher) with the problems of others, it is possible to stand back occasionally from immediate urgent demands and review the structural elements of the learning situation. One might, for example, begin by instituting just such a review as part of the regular structure—a quarterly or yearly long cool look! What aims need changing? What about a more economic use of time? Is routine activity X still worth the effort? Could area Y stand more attention? Does skill Z need some servicing?

Time lost on such occasional reflection might help to

reduce the masochistic unproductive drudgery which sometimes comes to be worn like a halo. Principles available to guide such structural reviews are scattered throughout the present book and throughout modern reports on the various sectors of education. As suggested in Chapter 3, one of the most important principles is to consider the individual human aspects of learning structure as well as general systematic aspects (timetables, learning programmes, 'psychology of learning', etc).

Policy for learning

One might sum up the last section as a recommendation to cultivate a conscious and deliberate policy for any learning situation, analysing the relevant factors and acting on those which are controllable. No doubt easier said than done! What policy might one suggest to a student who survived to this point in the text and wanted to know how he could best pursue further the study of human learning?

Perhaps the most obvious way would be to select one of the four chronological or educational stages discussed in the first four chapters and examine it more deeply. Deeper examination might mean following up some of the literature mentioned in the chapter or bibliography, perhaps relating the learning problems in greater detail to the developmental characteristics of that particular stage of life. One might skim through relevant books and periodicals in the library to collect empirical evidence for or against the arguments put forward. One might attempt to relate the arguments of the chapter to observations of, or practical experience with, actual learners of that age. One might make a more detailed comparison of the chosen stage with one of the other stages to see whether the tentative comparisons of the book can be developed or demolished. One might study whether it is really appropriate to study learning in stages, or, if so, in the particular stages chosen. And one might review the argument in relation to one particular subject of study or one particular method of learning or teaching.

Another way would be to look in detail at one particular approach to learning (behaviourist, sociological, philosophical, etc.) or one particular kind of evidence (experimental, 'clinical' common-sense, historical, etc.). But the most valuable next step may be to make a list of the problems about learning that seem interesting and then study one or two of these in depth. What are the respective roles of knowledge, skills, and attitudes in learning? How do the historically inherited institutions of learning (particular kinds of school, textbook, examination, etc.) foster or impede effective learning? How can an understanding of learning psychology be applied to improve one's own or other people's learning? (see McFarland, 1965, and Maddox, 1963). How far does learning depend on individual talent and application, and how far on establishing institutional structures that support and develop such personal characteristics? What is the relationship between scholastic skill and emotional development or involvement? Among all the causal factors determining learning processes what is the significance of individual responsibility for one's own learning?

What is the significance of what has come to be called 'educational technology' in learning—learning machines, language laboratories, mathematical apparatus, television, tape recorders, computors, and all such paraphernalia? What conclusions about learning are suggested by reading one of Professor B. F. Skinner's books, for example, *Cumulative Record*. How far can one justify Bruner's optimism about the possibility of teaching almost anything to anybody in some worthwhile form, provided that one evolves the appropriate structuring and presentation of the learning materials? Does it make sense to speak of 'mechanical' learning and 'creative' learning, and what exactly do these signify? (see Hudson, 1967). What exactly is 'transfer of training' or the 'discipline' of learning a subject—ideas which are frequently evoked when people are not clear about the express utility of some kind of learning and which, one feels, have some significance if only one could achieve a clearer formulation of what it is? How can one speed the destruction of institutional and intellectual obstacles to desirable change in learning? Why do many people cling to ignorant and biased views of learning when a considerable amount of substantial and reasonably validated knowledge has long been available to them?

If one considers further the role of child (or student), teacher, and culture in learning (as discussed briefly in chapter 3), what does one make of their interrelation? What is it and what should it be? Why do national styles in approach to learning persist with such tenacity despite a psychological framework which is, at least to some extent, international? Or can one detect a national emphasis even in schools of scientific psychology or sociology? Or are there signs of growing uniformity in learning policies among nations? What is the relative importance of psychological, sociological, historical, economic, political, or cultural factors in explaining different analyses of learning? And how do these factors bear upon the individual learner as well as on the learning institutions of any country?

These are some of the questions that might suggest a policy for the further study of learning as a human phenomenon. With any other topic to be studied or learned it is equally important to make a list of the questions that might be interesting to answer. This is the way to get a sense of general perspective and to give oneself a chance of picking out the really important questions. It is the way to develop a learning policy.

Conclusion

An introductory book like this can well conclude with questions rather than affirmations. Many questions have already been put in the preceding section, but one might end with a few of the most important general questions about learning that deserve constant study. What do we mean by 'learning'? What learning is most worthwhile and why? What methods of learning achieve various learning aims most economically, and what does 'economically' mean? What contextual factors (individual, social, administrative, political, etc) shape learning and how can one achieve increased control of them? What is distinctive about human learning?

Suggestions for further reading

Human learning is obviously a topic that ramifies widely—
in one direction into particular aspects of learning such as
learning to read, in the opposite direction into the whole
psychology of education and, indeed, of human behaviour.
The following suggestions about further reading must be
limited and partly arbitrary. In *Psychology and Teaching*
(Harrap, 1965) the author has already attempted to provide
a perspective on the general psychology of education, together with a bibliographical guide to further study. There
is no 'best buy' in further reading, for it depends on what
problems are selected for attack. If one absolutely had to
recommend a few books as being *generally* fruitful for the
study of learning and not too difficult, the choice might be
D. E. Broadbent's *Behaviour* (Methuen, 1964), S. Cotgrove's
The Science of Society (Allen and Unwin, 1967), E. Richardson's *The Environment of Learning* (Nelson, 1967), and possibly B. F. Skinner's *Cumulative Record* (Appleton-Century-
Crofts, 1959). But one would certainly not guarantee to
stick to this choice.

*1. Introduction: Some aspects of student learning and
some approaches to the analysis of learning*

Harry Maddox's paperback *How To Study* (Pan, 1963) and
118

A. Laing's booklet on *The Art of Study, Some Hints for Undergraduate Freshmen* (Leeds University Department of Education, 1964) are two handy introductions to practical aspects of student learning. Like other booklets in this category they cannot be expected to relieve a student of his own responsibility for self-understanding or for attending to the advice of tutors. Some students would find I. M. L. Hunter's *Memory, Facts and Fallacies* (Penguin, 1957) interesting and relevant. The literature on general aspects of higher learning is immense and sometimes practically illuminating. *Eighteen Plus—Unity and Diversity in Higher Education*, edited by Marjorie Reeves (Faber, 1965) and P. Marris's *The Experience of Higher Education* (Routledge, 1964) are interesting, while N. Sanford's *The American College* (Wiley, 1962) is one of the most important books on American higher education.

Further study of the main psychological approaches to learning really requires individual guidance into the deeper waters, but one might start by looking at D. E. Broadbent's *Behaviour* (Methuen, 1964) for a clear presentation of a behavioural scientist's point of view, E. H. Erikson's *Childhood and Society* (Penguin, 1965) for a social-psychoanalytical approach, and P. W. Musgrave's *The Sociology of Education* (Methuen, 1965) for a sociological approach. In the more or less behaviourist category one might add S. A. Mednick's *Learning* (Prentice-Hall, 1964)—a short and simple introduction to the experimental study of learning; W. F. Hill's *Learning, a Survey of Psychological Interpretations* (Methuen, 1964)—a clear exposition and comparison of psychological 'learning theories'; M. L. Bigge's *Learning Theories for Teachers* (Harper, 1964)—a possible alternative to, although not necessarily better for teachers than, Hill; W. H. Thorpe's *Learning and Instinct in Animals* (Methuen, 1956, 1963)—a substantial work which might repay at least dipping into to widen the biological horizons of the student of human learning; and B. F. Skinner's *Cumulative*

Record (Appleton-Century-Crofts, 1959) or one of his other books illustrating a concern more with the precise control of learning than with learning theory.

Along with Erikson one might mention J. A. C. Brown's *Freud and the Post-Freudians* (Penguin, 1961) for a lively and convenient review of diverse psychoanalytical viewpoints and Elizabeth Richardson's *The Environment of Learning* (Nelson, 1967) and *Group Study for Teachers* (Routledge, 1967) for a direct psychoanalytically oriented analysis of the group dynamics of certain actual learning situations. The bibliographies of these books lay their own trails of further reading. For a sociological approach, one might add S. Cotgrove's *The Science of Society* (Allen and Unwin, 1967), R. Frankenberg's *Communities in Britain* (Penguin, 1966), R. Fletcher's *The Family and Marriage in Britain* (Penguin, 1966), and T. B. Bottomore's *Sociology A Guide to Problems and Literature* (Unwin, 1962).

2. Pre-school learning

Here one might shortlist F. M. Hechinger's *Pre-School Education Today* (Doubleday, 1966), Melanie Klein's *Our Adult World and Its Roots in Infancy* (Tavistock, 1960), J. Bowlby's *Child Care and the Growth of Love* (Penguin, 1953) and J. and E. Newson's *Infant Care in an Urban Community* (Penguin, 1963). All four are thought-provoking but easy and interesting to read. One might add for further consideration Bernstein's article included in the Selected Bibliography of this book and any available account of how infants develop, whether A. Gesell's 'The Ontogenesis of Infant Behaviour' in L. Carmichael's *Manual of Child Psychology* (Chapman and Hall, 1954), R. S. Illingworth's *The Development of the Infant and Young Child* (Livingstone, 1963), or any other reasonably up-to-date account. The books by Hunt, Staats, and Stevenson, mentioned in chapter 2 are all substantial works but at least worth sampling in part or consulting in the library to get something of their flavour. Hunt gives a full account of Piaget's developmental psychology, although this can also be studied in J. H. Flavell's substantial, lucid and critical *The Developmental Psychology of Jean Piaget* (Van Nostrand, 1963), M. Brearley and E. Hitchfield's *A Teacher's Guide to Reading Piaget* (Routledge, 1966), or (sketchily) in Nathan Isaacs' pamphlet *The Growth of Understanding in the Young Child* (Ward Lock, 1961).

3. Primary school learning

The Plowden Report of 1967, as the bible of primary school learning in England, may be sufficient further reading for many, although, like *the* Bible, it may be read or acted upon only rarely and in very small pieces. General books that might help the student of primary school learning are John Blackie's *Inside the Primary School* (H.M.S.O., 1967), *The Formative Years* (B.B.C., 1968) by Gordon Trasler and others (although the latter book is concerned with early childhood in general), and the Scottish Education Department's Memorandum *Primary Education in Scotland* (H.M.S.O., 1965). L. G. W. Sealey and V. Gibbon's *Communication and Learning in the Primary School* (Blackwell, 1963) and P. Rance's *Teaching by Topics* (Ward Lock, 1968) are useful on their respective themes. Friedlander's article included in the Selected Bibliography offers a start to the critical examination of 'discovery learning'.

K. Lovell's *The Growth of Basic Mathematical and Scientific Concepts in Children* (University of London Press, 1962) is an interesting examination of how Piaget's principles operate in relation to parts of school learning. A. E. Tansley's *Reading and Remedial Reading* (Routledge, 1967), G. H. Hildreth's *Teaching Reading: A Guide to Basic Principles and Modern Practices* (Holt, 1958) and J. Downing's *The ita Symposium* (National Foundation for Educational Research,

1967) offer possible starting points on the huge literature of learning to read. *The Improvement of Reading* (McGraw-Hill, 4th edition, 1967) by R. M. Strang, C. M. McCullough, and A. E. Traxler is a substantial work that might be useful for reference or selective reading. M. F. Cleugh's *Teaching the Slow Learner in the Primary School* (Methuen, 1961) and Bristol University Institute of Education's *The Assessment and Education of Slow Learning Children* (University of London Press, 1967) are useful publications.

4. Secondary school learning

The Crowther Report *15 to 18* (H.M.S.O., 1959), although published in 1959, is still worth looking at, and perhaps particularly Part Six (pp. 313-403) on further education. This might be compared with Lady Venables' *The Young Worker at College* (Faber, 1967). The Newsom Report *Half Our Future* (H.M.S.O., 1963) is still important in relation to the secondary school children of average ability or less with whom it specially deals. E. A. Peel's *The Pupil's Thinking* (Oldbourne Press, 1960) illustrates Piaget's principles in relation to aspects of secondary schooling. *Discipline in Schools* (Pergamon, 1967) edited by L. Stenhouse discusses problems that sometimes impede secondary school learning and teaching. It might be studied by a group of students along with A. S. Neill's *Summerhill, A Radical Approach to Education* (Gollancz, 1964), M. Burn's *Mr. Lyward's Answer* (Hamilton, 1956), R. Farley's *Secondary Modern Discipline* (Black, 1960), J. Partridge's *Middle School* (Gollancz, 1966), and R. F. Mackenzie's *A Question of Living* (Collins, 1963).

E. B. Hurlock's *Adolescent Development* (McGraw-Hill, 3rd edition, 1967) is a substantial general study of adolescence and L. Hudson's *Contrary Imaginations* (Penguin, 1967) a study of different kinds of intellectual style or capacity. The Schools Council's *The Educational Implications of Social and Economic Change* (H.M.S.O., 1967) is a most varied and stimulating booklet on different aspects of the topic indicated. E. Richardson's *The Environment of Learning* (Nelson, 1967) has already been commended and is particularly relevant to secondary school learning. M. F. Cleugh has a volume on *Teaching the Slow Learner in the Secondary School* (Methuen, 1961).

5. Some learning problems

Suggestions for reading are included in the chapter itself. The best further advice one can give is (1) to make full use of tutors and librarians by consulting them, (2) to browse in libraries and bookshops, and (3) to find out and consult regularly educational periodicals which sift out promising publications and developments (e.g. *Educational Research, British Journal of Educational Studies, British Journal of Educational Psychology, Education for Teaching*). The great volume of publication makes it a prime necessity for tutors to instruct their students and perhaps themselves in the practical arts of finding and using learning resources.

Select Bibliography

AIKEN, W. M. (1942), *The Story of the Eight-Year Study*, New York, Harper

ARGYLE, M. (1967), *The Psychology of Interpersonal Behaviour*, Penguin Books

BERNE, E. (1966), *Games People Play*, Deutsch

BERNSTEIN, B. (1961), 'Social Class and Linguistic Development: A Theory of Social Learning', pp. 288-314 of Halsey, Floud and Anderson's *Education, Economy and Society*, New York, The Free Press of Glencoe

BERGER, P. L. (1966), *Invitation to Sociology*, Penguin Books

BIGGE, M. L. (1964), *Learning Theories for Teachers*, Harper International Student Reprints

BLACKIE, J. (1967), *Inside the Primary School*, H.M.S.O.

BLYTH, W. A. L. (1965), *English Primary Education, A Sociological Description*, Routledge & Kegan Paul

BOTTOMORE, T. B. (1962), *Sociology, A Guide to Problems and Literature*, Unwin

BOWLBY, J. (1953), *Child Care and the Growth of Love*, Penguin Books

BREARLEY, M. and HITCHFIELD, E. (1966), *A Teacher's Guide to Reading Piaget*, Routledge & Kegan Paul

BRISTOL UNIVERSITY INSTITUTE OF EDUCATION (1967), *The Assessment and Education of Slow Learning Children*, University of London Press

BROADBENT, D. E. (1964), *Behaviour*, Methuen

BRUNER, J. S. (1961), *The Process of Education*, Harvard University Press

BRUNER, J. S. (1962), *On Knowing*, Harvard University Press

BURN, M. (1956), *Mr. Lyward's Answer*, Hamilton

124

CARMICHAEL, L. (1954), *Manual of Child Psychology*, Chapman and Hall

CLEUGH, M. F. (1961), *Teaching the Slow Learner in the Primary School*, Methuen

CLEUGH, M. F. (1961), *Teaching the Slow Learner in the Secondary School*, Methuen

CONNELL, W. F., DEBUS, R. L., and NIBLETT, W. R. (editors) (1967), *Readings in the Foundations of Education*, Routledge & Kegan Paul

COTGROVE, S. (1967), *The Science of Society*, Allen & Unwin

CROWTHER, LORD (1959), *15 to 18*, H.M.S.O.

DOWNING, J. (1967), *The ita Symposium*, National Foundation for Educational Research

DOUGLAS, J. W. B. (1958), *Children Under Five*, Allen & Unwin

DOUGLAS, J. W. B. (1966), *The Home and the School, A Study of Ability and Attainment in the Primary School*, Macgibbon & Kee

ERIKSON, E. H. (1965), *Childhood and Society*, Penguin Books

FARLEY, R. (1960), *Secondary Modern Discipline*, Black

FLAVELL, J. H. (1963), *The Developmental Psychology of Jean Piaget*, Van Nostrand

FLETCHER, R. (1966), *The Family and Marriage in Britain*, Penguin Books

FOSS, B. (1967), *Education as Art, Science and Technology*, Harrap

FRANKENBERG, R. (1966), *Communities in Britain, Social Life in Town and Country*, Penguin Books

FRIEDLANDER, B. Z. (1965), 'A Psychologist's Second Thoughts on Concepts, Curiosity and Discovery in Teaching', Harvard Educational Review, Vol. 35, No. 1

GARDNER, D. E. M. (1966), *Experiment and Tradition in Primary Schools*, Methuen

HADOW, Sir W. H. (1931), *The Primary School*, H.M.S.O.

HECHINGER, F. M. (1966), *Pre-School Education Today*, New York, Doubleday

HILDRETH, G. H. (1958), *Teaching Reading: A Guide to Basic Principles and Modern Practices*, New York, Holt

HILL, W. F. (1964), *Learning, A Survey of Psychological Interpretations*, Methuen

HUDSON, L. (1967), *Contrary Imaginations*, Penguin Books

HUNT, J. M. (1961), *Intelligence and Experience*, New York, Ronald Press

HUNTER, I. M. L. (1957), *Memory, Facts and Fallacies*, Penguin Books

HURLOCK, E. B. (1967), *Adolescent Development*, 3rd edition, McGraw-Hill

ILLINGWORTH, R. S. (1963), *The Development of the Infant and Young Child*, Edinburgh, Livingstone

ISAACS, N. (1961), *The Growth of Understanding in the Young Child*, Ward Lock

KLEIN, J. (1961), *Working With Groups, The Social Psychology of Discussion and Decision*, Hutchinson

KLEIN, J. (1965), *Samples from English Cultures*, Routledge & Kegan Paul

KLEIN, M. (1960), *Our Adult World and Its Roots in Infancy*, Tavistock Publications

LAING, A. (1964), *The Art of Study, Some Hints for Undergraduate Freshmen*, Leeds University Department of Education

LEITH, G. O. M. (1966), *A Handbook of Programmed Learning*, University of Birmingham

LINDGREN, H. C. (1962), *Educational Psychology in the Classroom*, New York, Wiley International Editions

LORENZ, K. (1966), *On Aggression*, Methuen

LOVELL, K. (1967), *Team Teaching*, Leeds University Institute of Education

LOVELL, K. (1962), *The Growth of Basic Mathematical and Scientific Concepts in Children*, University of London Press

MCFARLAND, H. S. N. (1965), *Psychology and Teaching*, Harrap

MACKENZIE, R. F. (1963), *A Question of Living*, Collins

MADDOX, H. (1963), *How To Study*, Pan Books

MARRIS, P. (1964), *The Experience of Higher Education*, Routledge & Kegan Paul

MEDNICK, S. A. (1964), *Learning*, Englewood Cliffs, New Jersey, Prentice-Hall

MUSGRAVE, P. W. (1965), *The Sociology of Education*, Methuen

MUSSEN, P. H., CONGER, J. J., and KAGAN, J. (1965), *Child Development and Personality*, Harper & Row

MUSSEN, P. H., CONGER, J. J., and KAGAN, J. (1965), *Readings in Child Development and Personality*, Harper & Row

NEILL, A. S. (1964), *Summerhill, A Radical Approach to Education*, Gollancz

NEWMAN, H. H., FREEMAN, R. N., and HOLZINGER, K. J. (1937), *Twins: A Study of Heredity and Environment*, Chicago University Press

NEWSOM, Sir J. (1963), *Half Our Future*, H.M.S.O.

NEWSON, J. and E. (1963), *Infant Care in an Urban Community*, Penguin Books

PARTRIDGE, J. (1966), *Middle School*, Gollancz

PEEL, E. A. (1960), *The Pupil's Thinking*, Oldbourne

PETERS, R. S. (1958), *The Concept of Motivation*, Routledge & Kegan Paul

PETERS, R. S. (1966), *Ethics and Education*, Allen & Unwin

PETERS, R. S. (editor) (1967), *The Concept of Education*, Allen & Unwin

PLOWDEN, LADY (1967), *Children and Their Primary Schools*, H.M.S.O.

RANCE, P. (1968), *Teaching by Topics*, Ward Lock

REDL, H. B. (1964), *Soviet Educators on Soviet Society*, London, Collier-Macmillan

REEVES, M. (editor) (1965), *Eighteen Plus—Unity and Diversity in Higher Education*, Faber

RICHARDSON, E. (1967), *The Environment of Learning, Conflict and Understanding in the Secondary School*, Nelson

RICHARDSON, E. (1967), *Group Study for Teachers*, Routledge & Kegan Paul

SANFORD, N. (1962), *The American College, a Psychological and Social Interpretation of the Higher Learning*, New York, J. Wiley

SCHOOLS COUNCIL (1967), *The Educational Implications of Social and Economic Change*, Working Paper No. 12, H.M.S.O.

SCOTTISH EDUCATION DEPARTMENT (1946), *Primary Education*, H.M.S.O.

SCOTTISH EDUCATION DEPARTMENT (1965), *Primary Education in Scotland*, H.M.S.O.

SEALEY, L. G. W. and GIBBON, V. (1963), *Communication and Learning in the Primary School*, Blackwell

SKINNER, B. F. (1959), *Cumulative Record*, New York, Appleton-Century-Crofts

STAATS, A. W. (editor), (1964), *Human Learning, Studies Extending Conditioning Principles to Complex Behavior*, Holt, Rinehart and Winston

STENHOUSE, L. and others (1967), *Discipline in Schools*, Pergamon

STEVENSON, H. W. (editor), (1967), *Early Behavior, Comparative and Developmental Approaches*, John Wiley

STRANG, R. M., MCCULLOUGH, C. M., and TRAXLER, C. E. (1967), *The Improvement of Reading*, 4th edition, McGraw-Hill

TANSLEY, A. E. (1967), *Reading and Remedial Reading*, Routledge & Kegan Paul

THORPE, W. H. (1963), *Learning and Instinct in Animals*, Methuen

TIBBLE, J. W. (1966), *The Study of Education*, Routledge & Kegan Paul

TRASLER, G. and others (1968), *The Formative Years*, B.B.C.

VENABLES, LADY (1967), *The Young Worker*, Faber

WALLER, W. (1932), *The Sociology of Teaching*, New York, J. Wiley

WOODWORTH, R. S. (1940), *Psychology*, Methuen